# Italian Westerns: The Essential Films

## Stephen Hoover

# Contents

# Intro

Spaghetti westerns. When many people think of them, it's likely that visions of low budgets and badly dubbed lines go through their heads. People who have explored this genre know better.

Spaghetti westerns took what Americans expected to see in a western and completely flipped it around. The heroes were no longer examples of shining virtue, they were downright dangerous and oftentimes criminals themselves.

The look of these films also reinvented the image of the frontier. While American westerns had spectacular examples of cinematography to their credit, they tended to show the sheer beauty of the Western U.S. The colorful mesas, endless skies and the untamed potential they represented became iconic. In Italian westerns, mostly shot in Spain (which does very well as a double for the Southwest U.S.), the landscapes were different. They were harsh, bleak, dusty, windy and scorched by the sun.

The charming western towns were replaced by villages with featureless buildings, bleached by the sun until they were as white as the bones they were sometimes surrounded by. Many of the villages and towns seemed, right from the first glance, to be where people went to die more than where they went to live.

The music in these movies is as memorable as the films themselves. Ennio Morricone brought electric guitars, wailing voices and eerie, abstract sounds to the western soundtrack, transforming it into something entirely new. In his hands, the sound of the West became haunting, sometimes frightening and sometimes epic beyond belief.

All of these things together created a genre that came and went relatively quickly, but that had an impact that is still felt today. Some of Hollywood's biggest directors—including Quentin Tarantino—are huge fans of some of these films. In fact, some of the films, such as *The Good, the Bad and the Ugly* and *Once Upon a Time in the West* are regarded as among the finest films ever made, regardless of genre.

This book will give some background information on these films, followed by some examples that are worth seeing. They are not necessarily the best of the best where these movies are concerned, but taken together, they demonstrate the hallmarks of this genre in memorable ways and, if one wished to explore further, they would help develop a better and more substantial understanding of the genre.

To write only about the best films in this genre would restrict the films to those of a handful of directors and not take in the incredible variety that is to be found among these films. From unforgettable characters such as Django and the Man with No Name to actors that practically made a career out of playing a particular type of character, such as Lee Van Cleef, there is a lot to take away from these films. You'll find the performances in some of these films to be surprisingly good, full of depth and full of room for interpretation. You'll find incredible camerawork that was done on tight budgets and risky storytelling that makes some of these films shocking at times. You'll find wonderful moments of creativity where, somehow, a film full of actors who spoke several different languages that was being made by underfunded crews on sets and at locations that were picked because they were affordable rather than ideal, all come together in a way that's something you'll never forget, and the influence of which you'll see throughout modern films.

# Chapter 1

## Reimagining the West and the Western Film

There are few things as American as the stories, myths, legends and history of the American West. The time period during which the U.S. was expanding into what is now the Western and Southwestern United States has been a consistently fertile ground for filmmakers, with early western films mostly painting a romantic, adventurous and nostalgic picture of the time period.

Then, the Italians came along.

During the 1960s and into the 1970s, the classic era of films that were to become known as spaghetti westerns was in full swing. These films offered something different than American audiences had seen before. Take the darkness and cynicism of the most intense film noir and the violence of the most powerful war movies, and combine it with a decidedly de-romanticized vision of the Old West and you get the basic ingredients for a spaghetti western.

The term "spaghetti western" was originally something of a pejorative. In Italy itself, these are called Italian westerns, but the term "spaghetti western" has long since lost its insulting edge. Today, these films have garnered a large cult following and have influenced many of the westerns and even other types of films that came after them.

## A Different Vision of the West

It's unlikely there are many people out there who haven't seen at least one spaghetti western in their lives. The brilliant *The Good, the Bad and the Ugly* is likely the one that most people are familiar with, even if they're not familiar with other films of the genre.

These films tend to be much darker than their American counterparts are. In these westerns, the frontier is something to be respected and sometimes feared rather than conquered. There are some very refreshing elements in these movies, however, that will likely be welcomed by those unfamiliar with the genre but familiar with the American western films and television shows of the 1950s and 1960s.

## A More Diverse Range of Characters

You'll see far fewer Native Americans in spaghetti westerns than you will in American westerns. When they do show up on-screen, however, how they're portrayed may sometimes be a welcome surprise for the audience. Native Americans were oftentimes portrayed as cruel savages or, in the most uncomfortable older American westerns, as buffoons. When they do pop up in spaghetti westerns, the treatment tends to be more respectful. They might be a force to be feared or a people to be admired, but they're people.

*Navajo Joe* features a portrayal of Native Americans that is much more positive than one might have seen in an American film. In this film, Joe—played by Burt Reynolds, who claims some Native American ancestry—could be any western character. He's seeking revenge, he's a dangerous fighter and he has no compunction about killing someone who's done him a wrong. He exists in a world of moral ambiguity and is well-suited to surviving in it. If you think he's a primitive buffoon or someone to be romanticized, you're sorely mistaken, and you just might pay dearly for that underestimation.

Where the minstralism of some American westerns is strongly contrasted with spaghetti westerns, however, is in the portrayal of Mexicans. Because he appears in one of the most well-known films of this genre, Tuco Ramirez from *The Good, the Bad and the Ugly* provides a good example.

Tuco could have been another sidekick or Mexican buffoon. He had the accent, he talks incessantly and he comes off as something of a small-time hood. This is probably the deadliest thing about him; he gets people to underestimate him. To paraphrase one of his most famous lines, if you underestimate the man, you understand nothing about Tuco. He's just as lethal as anyone else in the film and, in fact, more of a force to be reckoned with than most. Given that no one in this film is really a good guy, so to speak, Tuco is free to develop as a character alongside, rather than as a sidekick to, the white protagonist.

Spaghetti westerns sometimes incorporated political elements into them and, given that they were European, the politics are different than one might expect from an American film. In American films, the characters were generally looking West, out to tame the frontier and bring the glory of Western civilization to the plains, mountains and deserts that they made their new homes. In spaghetti westerns, the messiness of politics is oftentimes on full display and the greed and idiocy that drive some conflicts are used very effectively to add depth to the story.

Look for Mexican bandits in these films who are really the good guys or, as these films tend to eschew such nice and neat morality, at least the better guys. Films such as *Requiescant* from 1967 very much celebrate the revolutionary spirit that founded modern Mexico, for example. Rather than casting the West as a place where noble Americans fought savage Native tribes and bloodthirsty Mexican bandits, these films weren't afraid to delve into the complexities involved in late 19th century frontier politics and society.

## Budgets

These films are not known for having large budgets. Nonetheless, the directors oftentimes managed to capture both the beauty and the ugliness of the West in ways that American westerns sometimes struggled with. Rather than yet another scene of a cowboy galloping through Monument Valley, these films oftentimes show wide-screen wastelands, with no towns for miles. The deserts in these films are as deadly and capricious as the people who inhabit them. The land is gorgeous in some scenes, but there is always some menace to it. There's no law here. Entire towns can turn into battlefields in the space of a day or, sometimes, an hour.

With these low budgets, storytelling is sometimes amplified, it would seem. The actors have it upon them to make the film worth watching. They clomp around on rickety Western sets, mostly located in Italy, and the low-budget sets sometimes add to the authenticity of the scenes. Grime, dust, grease and filth are common on the screen. The cowboys, if they had white hats, would be covered in dust soon enough. In fact, in these films, there's a good chance that they're not even cowboys. They're killers and thieves who just happen to be wearing cowboy-style hats.

In a spaghetti western, one is far more likely to be involved in a scene because they feel enveloped in the West rather than because they're wowed with the budgets. The shots usually say something in these films. An expansive shot of an endless vista is not there merely to impress, but to inform. What they inform the audience of is that there is real danger here and one never knows when they're about to meet their end.

## The Pure Enjoyment

If a hero gets shot off of his horse in an American western, you know he's going to be acting the part of an injured guy for at least a few scenes, most likely. If someone gets shot off of a horse in a spaghetti western, they're probably dead. That may sound like morbid cause for enjoyment, but this type of peril is what makes these films worth watching.

Anyone can die in these films. Bullets are real. Lances and arrows are real. The desert is real. Characters don't have to gun down a horde of adversaries to prove that they're tough—though they do, in quite a few cases—because merely surviving a day in this world is proof enough.

When watching the films featured in the second half of this book, realize that these are westerns for grownups. These aren't singing cowboys or heroic gunfighters who roll into town and make everything right. Watch the painful death of a soldier in *The Good, the Bad and the Ugly* to see a stark contrast with the clutch-your-chest-and-grimace deaths that characterized the westerns that came before the Italians left their mark.

In these movies, people sometimes die horribly, far from home, far from comfort and the best they can hope for is a few drags off a cigarette from a nameless bandit to ease their suffering. These films aren't just about the West and the legends that were born out of it. They're about people living—and dying—in the West, and they've spawned entirely new legends purely because of their memorable characters, stories and outstanding executions as pieces of art.

These films have left their mark, to be certain. From the much darker westerns that flowed out of Hollywood in later years, such as *The Unforgiven,* to the barely-speaking heroes of films like *The Road Warrior,* to reinventions of the genre such as *Django Unchained,* these films matter. The term "spaghetti western" is not only no longer a pejorative, it's a compliment.

Get ready for an intense ride, because the films to come will make you reconsider your notions of the Old West and the people who called it home.

As one last note: Crank the sound when watching these films. The music in these movies tends to be stellar, and it's worth a book in its own right.

# Chapter 2:

# The Style

There are distinct differences between the styles of Italian westerns and most of the American westerns that preceded them. The primary difference that a first-time viewer will likely notice is simply visual. The West, in Italian films, will look familiar to anyone who actually lives in the West, even in modern times. The landscapes are dusty and barren. Being outside for any length of time, at least in Southwest desert climes, is likely to result in being covered in dust and, over time, developing lines on the face from sunburn and squinting.

The Hollywood westerns with which viewers were familiar before Italian directors took the genre in an entirely new direction were much different in terms of how they looked, and some of the specific differences carry through in the plots, characters and other elements that make these films.

## Contrasts with American Westerns

Watch American westerns and you'll get the idea that the frontier was a place where dreams come true. All one had to do was stake out some land to homestead, join a cattle train and have the gumption to take on hordes of hostile natives, who invariably fell like rows of wheat before revolvers and Winchesters.

In Italian westerns, the West is not so kind.

From the stark and barren landscapes of *The Good, the Bad and the Ugly* to the avenging Native warrior in *Navajo Joe*, the West in Italian cinema is rich, dark and deadly. This is a place where dreams may come true, but those who seek their dreams through toil and perseverance, more often than not, end up filthy, poor and victimized by bandits who would rather take than create. Gunslingers in these films don't open up with their .45s to make things right; they do it for revenge or for personal gain. When they do try to make things right, it's usually a diversion from their typical enterprises of making themselves wealthier and more powerful.

These stories are epic in nature. To have a truly epic story, there needs to be darkness. Darkness is as abundant in these films as open space is in the West.

The film that's generally regarded as the one that launched the craze for spaghetti westerns is the 1964 Sergio Leone classic *A Fistful of Dollars*. It sets the tone, to be certain, and for demonstrating the contrasts between American and Italian westerns, it provides an excellent reference. This film features a hero who is certainly not a white-hat type and a plot that is complex, dark and full of deadly characters.

These films, however, tend to feature some common elements in terms of the settings and, quite often, the settings themselves function as a sort of character.

## Violence

To get a good idea of the difference between American westerns and Italian westerns, the scene in *A Fistful of Dollars* where the Man with No Name asks the local undertaker to get "three coffins ready" is instructional.

The scene opens up not unlike something one would expect to see in an American western. The protagonist rides into town and is immediately harassed by a gang of thugs. They insult him and, eventually, start taking shots at his mule's feet, sending the animal into a panic and forcing the Man with No Name to dismount by grabbing onto a signpost. He casually gets down and walks over to the men, now four in number.

The Man with No Name makes no speech about driving the ruffians out of town, doesn't tell them that there's new sheriff in town and doesn't engage in any other good-guy clichés. The Man with No Name demands that men apologize, to his mule. His mule doesn't like it when people are laughing at him.

The Man with No Name is not a force of justice. He's a predator and he's toying with his prey.

The western quick-draw sequence ensues, but it's different than one might expect if they were accustomed to John Wayne westerns. The Man with No Name guns down all four of the ruffians without breaking a sweat. He wastes no shots and leaves no survivors. The local sheriff threatens to have the Man with No Name strung up, and the Man With no Name admonishes the sheriff to get the bodies in the ground. He apologizes to the coffin maker, the Man with No Name admitting that it was his mistake to ask for three coffins, and that he should have asked for four.

In *Django*, there's a fine example of how the violence in these movies differs from that portrayed in American movies, and it involves one of the classic movie tropes: the damsel in distress.

Poor Maria finds herself being whipped by a group of banditos. Django watches, seemingly impassively, as it goes on, but a group of cowboys wearing red scarves steps in and kills all of the banditos.

Unfortunately, for Maria, they intend to tie her to a cross and burn her to death. Django is not having it.

He's different from the Man with No Name, seemingly friendlier and more passive, but he has the same cold eyes. He casually guns down the cowboys and offers Maria his protection. As she considers it, one of the cowboys starts crawling across the ground and Django executes the cowboy as casually as someone might stomp on a roach.

The violence in these movies oftentimes has this tinge of brutality to it that makes it more real, more visceral and more frightening. The heroes aren't gunslingers who are skilled and deadly because of their moral superiority. In fact, there's usually an element of psychopathy to their characters that gives them the coldness necessary to kill without hesitation, remorse or, for that matter, fail.

*The Good, the Bad and the Ugly* features one of the most powerful portrayals of violence in the West and in one of its most distinctive scenarios: the shootout. In this shootout, it's not the gunplay that gets the audience's attention, but the lead-up to it. A seemingly endless sequence of Angel Eyes, Tuco and Blondie (the Man with No Name) staring each other down somehow never loses its tension, even when it seems like it's already gone on far too long.

In an Italian western, characters don't face justice or villainy when they're looking down a six-shooter; they face death. The audience is always aware of this. Sometimes, the action has the feel that one would expect in any action movie. It's cathartic or even thrilling to watch. In other cases, it's brutal, such as Maria being whipped. In all cases, however, it's consequential. These films might squint a bit at violence—or at least the characters do—but they don't flinch.

Later films took what the Italian directors set up and added a lot more depth. In *The Unforgiven*, for example, the violence is not cathartic. It's as brutal and unceremonious as slaughtering a cow and the audience experiences it through the reaction of the characters and the remorse that they carry with them.

## More Graphic, More Realistic

If you thought torture scenes didn't get real until *Reservoir Dogs* came around, you're mistaken. Italian westerns were famous—or notorious—for their violence. *Django* features a brutal scene where a man gets his ear cut off—it happens on-screen, it's not implied—and then shot in the back as he stumbles away. *Navajo Joe* climaxes with a shootout in a cemetery where the baddest of the bad guys sheds his mortal coil courtesy of a thrown axe in the forehead, after enduring a brutal beating at the hands of the protagonist.

While many of the violent sequences in these films are quite graphic, Leone's violence tends to be distinctive. He oftentimes uses long lead-ups to the violence, increasing the tension. The aforementioned scene in *A Fistful of Dollars* is characteristic of his style. As the Man with No Name confronts the four thugs in the town, there is a series of long pauses, shots of their guns, shots of the Man with No Name squinting. There's even a sequence where one of the bad guys spits and the Man with No Name's eyes follow it to the ground.

Leone's violence is mirrored in other films, where the lead-ups oftentimes involve silent sequences where music plays over the top, oftentimes with a strained, nearly operatic voice or some other very prominent musical motif holding the viewer's attention.

At the end of *Navajo Joe*, the protagonist sits in the graveyard, music playing over the top of the sequence. He's injured badly, but he's completed his mission. In many of these films, completing an important task leads right to the graveyard, whether one is doing the burying or being buried themselves.

The violence, while graphic, is often committed by men who are downright professional about it. In *Death Rides a Horse*, Meceita wants to ride with Ryan to get vengeance for his family. Ryan tells him no, saying that Meceita has "too much hate" in him. While righteous anger might drive some protagonists in these films to exact revenge, they're generally very cool when it comes to actually committing the murders that they seek. This is a cynical world and, in such a world, it's best not to be too attached to one's ego. In fact, in that same sequence, Ryan speaks of settling accounts, placing revenge in the same category as accountancy, for all practical purposes, at least for Ryan himself.

## Tools of War

In westerns, six-shooters are as much a part of wardrobe as boots and cowboy hats. There are some anachronisms and outright mistakes in these movies in regards to the hardware that the heroes and villains carry, but most of them make for interesting viewing.

In *A Fistful of Dollars*, Blondie (the Man with No Name) doesn't carry the gun usually associated with heroes in American westerns, the Colt Peacemaker. These guns were .45 Long Colt chambered six-shooters that are seen in the hands of many movie protagonists. In *Gunfight at the O.K. Corral*, all the protagonists carry them. They do appear in Italian western films—appropriately, since they were common sidearms of the era—but there are some interesting tropes with guns in these films that make them distinctive.

Blondie carries a Colt 1851 Navy revolver. This firearm, originally designed to use percussion caps and balls, were converted to fire cartridge ammunition quite frequently in the years following the Civil War. Blondie's—even though the war is still going on during the film—is already converted. A military weapon is just not quite deadly enough for this protagonist.

Tuco is even more interesting. A scene in a gun shop takes significant liberties where realism is concerned, but the result is one of the better scenes involving a western antihero. Tuco can't find the gun he wants, so he takes pieces of various guns and fashions them into something that suits him much better. He has a signature weapon. Fitting, given that he's one of the most distinctive killers in all western movies, American or Italian. His building of a custom weapon also demonstrates that this character has killed enough to know exactly what works best for him.

Winchester repeating rifles are big, of course. Ramon from *A Fistful of Dollars* uses one as his signature weapon. Of course, once the Man with No Name guns down everyone, Ramon is proven wrong. A man with a .45 meeting a man with a rifle, sometimes, does win.

You're not going to see the same type of emphasis on hero weapons in these films that you would in many American westerns. Don't expect silver bullets or shining six-shooters. What you will see are killers who have tools that they prefer for the job and, just as a good carpenter prefers a saw that cuts well, these killers prefer weapons that cut their opposition down, whether it's a rifle, a pistol, a Gatling gun or something they built themselves on the spot.

## Violence Has Consequences

Revenge stories are nothing new for westerns, but the stories in Italian westerns tend to be very dark and ambiguous where seeking vengeance is concerned. The protagonists oftentimes rack up a very high body count—sometimes higher than the villain's—in the course of seeking vengeance.

*Django* is a good example of this. Django doesn't ride into town on a white horse seeking to bring the law to a forgotten berg in the middle of a wasteland. He drags a coffin around with him. He doesn't get his final revenge by fan-shooting a gleaming six-gun; he uses a cross in a graveyard to depress the trigger, his hands destroyed.

In many of these films, the violence keeps coming, but so do the consequences for that violence. There isn't as much righteous violence as one would expect in these films. When the Man with No Name guns down Ramon, it's really two criminals having it out, not a good guy vs. bad guy throwdown at high noon.

This tends to give these films a more realistic quality, in many regards. Violence is to be feared in these films. Helpless people— villagers, farmers, young women—are oftentimes brutalized in these films, but these characters don't have their entire futures solved for them when the hero comes into town. More often than not, if a protagonist in these films rescues someone from bandits or other thugs, it's because he has a beef with one of them, not because he's seeking to set everything right in the world.

## Nobody Wins

"Happily ever after" seldom occurs in these movies. In most cases, the protagonist will somehow get what they're after, but the endings aren't so clean-cut as to be actually happy, in these cases. The body count that usually precedes the hero getting what they want oftentimes offsets the victory.

*The Great Silence* is a particularly good example of this. The film is featured later in the book, but suffice it to say that the ending will leave most audiences a bit shocked out and, likely, with a different impression of the way violence can play out in this genre.

By the end of these films, expect the protagonist to be brutalized, beaten, bloody and probably shot at least once. You don't get out of these gunfights without doing your fair share of suffering and anyone who thinks this is the safe, Nerf-covered frontier featured in popular American westerns has another thing coming. These films are intentionally brutal, but they tend to have more depth to them because of that.

There are some small measures of hope in these films, however. The ending of *The Good, the Bad and the Ugly* is a particularly good example. A little act of loyalty—if not exactly friendship—at the end of the film prevents the protagonist from being an outright villain, but the margin between him being a villain and a hero is as narrow as his final target in the film.

## Themes

Some of the protagonists in these films are very dark, very tormented and their being good or bad is not exactly clear-cut. In fact, these films are at their best when the heroes are just as shady as the villains; the heroes just happen to have a sliver of morality that differentiates them.

A fine example of this is found in *The Good, the Bad and the Ugly*. Any one of these guys could fit any one of those titles. They all embody them at various times. Angel Eyes, however, is the worst of the lot, so he fits in the middle. The Man with No Name—called Blondie here—is supposedly the good, but he's a bandit, a killer and about as quick to pull a gun as anyone could be. Tuco is the ugly, but he's capable of being loyal and certainly capable of being bad.

Nothing is easy in these films as far as picking the hero goes. It's usually left up to the audience to identify with the person who's followed the closest in the story or who, at least, seems the most likely to survive. Essentially, rather than seeing one's self as riding alongside a hero and taking out the bad guys, the audience can identify with these characters based on who would be most likely to get them through the ordeal. Angel Eyes would kill you as soon as you became inconvenient. Tuco wouldn't go out of his way to help anyone, and don't double-cross him, but he can be a good person when you need someone to have your back. Blondie is the most likeable character, even showing mercy to a dying solider who he doesn't even know—another man without a name caught up in a senseless procession of violence.

## Not Good, Not Bad, but Sardonic

The protagonist, who is usually the most lethal character of all in these films, oftentimes has a very sardonic quality to them. There are great lines in the movies that are usually the precursors to someone getting shot or otherwise taken out. The classic line "You brought two too many," delivered by Charles Bronson in *Once Upon a Time in the West*. Is a fine example. Faced with three deadly assassins, he asks if they brought a horse for him. They have three, and one of the assassins, predictably, remarks that they didn't bring enough.

They brought two too many, just as Bronson says.

Eastwood was excellent at making his characters the epitome of sardonic. He taunts Ramon at the end of *A Fistful of Dollars*, flatly telling Ramon to aim for the heart after the Man with No Name gets up over and over again after apparently being shot in the heart repeatedly.

In these films, expect some of the best lines to be delivered when someone is about to get what's coming to them. There are some great comedy moments in these films that are rather subtle, as well. For instance, when Tuco struggles to read the word "idiots" in a letter in *The Good, the Bad and the Ugly*, Blondie helps him and then specifies that the letter is for Tuco.

The sardonic nature of many of the characters oftentimes serves to reinforce their overall ambiguity from a moral standpoint. These people are so accustomed to death and destruction that they literally crack jokes in the face of it. What makes it a source of ambiguity is that you're as likely to find such a dark sense of humor among a group of ER nurses as you are among a group of hardened criminals. People with different backgrounds and intentions use this type of humor to get through some of the worst in life, whether they're helping those desperately in need or doing something quite the opposite.

**Complex Conflicts**

The Mexican Revolution was a long, complex war that mirrored many of the revolutions fought in other nations during the early years of the 20th century. The conflict began with a rebellion against Porfirio Diaz by Francisco I. Madero, beginning in 1910. There were more than two sides in this revolution, making it even more complex historically and politically than most. The revolution is most often dated as lasting between 1910 and 1920, though echoes of the conflict continued until nearly the 1930s.

While the rule of Diaz was characterized by significant industrial advancement and modernization, it was also a time when civil rights were nearly non-existent. Political corruption was the norm and, among the rural population and others who found themselves outside the tiny percentage of Mexicans who controlled the majority of the nation's wealth and resources, the urge for political change took hold.

This led to the emergence of revolutionary leaders whose fame spread across borders and oceans. Diaz had made it virtually impossible for the peasant class to own the land on which they worked and most of them lived in crushing poverty, under the thumb of a ruler who believed that he was the best man to rule Mexico, and one who had no tolerance for opposition.

## The Problems Start

When the election in 1910 came around, Diaz expected himself to take it handily. He had already established a norm of rigging elections or intimidating the citizens into voting for him whenever necessary, but he expected that he would take the presidency in 1910 without having to engage in anything illegal. When it became apparent to Diaz that his reformist opposition, Madero, was going to take the election, he resorted to familiar, oppressive tactics.

Madero found himself under arrest for planning to overthrow the government, a charge which was trumped up. Diaz went ahead and rigged the elections, ensuring his win. Madero came from a wealthy family, so it wasn't long before he was out of jail on bail and fled to Texas.

The phony charges against Madero, that he was planning an armed rebellion, became a reality after Diaz claimed the presidency as a result of his rigged election. Madero went ahead and called for an armed revolution, and it came.

This led to the rising of heroes that remain popular figures in Mexican and American history. Pancho Villa, Emiliano Zapata and other charismatic and effective leaders gathered armies of peasants under them and began rising up against the wealthy landowners, corrupt politicians and bullying military that had oppressed them for so long.

As is the case in many Italian westerns, it wasn't always clear who the good guys and bad guys were in this revolution. It's generally noted that Orozco, a popular revolutionary leader who once drew tens of thousands of people to the street to cheer him when he returned to Chihuahua, sought political power in the Madero government following the revolution, found himself in conflict with Madero and ended up giving up his government position, including an offer for a governorship of Chihuahua.

Orozco would end up living in exile, and eventually house arrest, in the U.S., but continued to ferment revolution in Mexico. He was killed by U.S. forces after being identified as a horse thief while on his way back to Mexico to fight against the government.

Emiliano Zapata—the man for whom the subgenre of spaghetti westerns is named—is one of the most famous faces of the Mexican revolution. He led a peasant uprising starting in the state of Morelos.

Zapata and his army, the Zapatistas, were instrumental in the ousting of Diaz. He was able to organize very large armies of peasants and was a popular leader. While Zapata was vital in the success of the revolution, Madero failed to embrace him. Following Madero's ascent to power, the Zapatista army soon found itself in conflict with the Zapatistas.

Zapata supported redistributing the land to the oppressed peasant class, making him a hero to the people in whose name the Mexican revolution—ostensibly—was being fought. He was an ally of Pancho Villa and the two of them are still regarded as allies of the people and leaders who stood up against the oppression of the landless classes.

Francisco "Pancho" Villa is another famous name from this time period. He was a bandit in the northern portion of Mexico who became a military leader. He eventually ascended to the level of governor of Chihuahua. His political leanings mirrored those of his ally Emiliano Zapata. Like Zapata, Villa would take over the large hacienda estates in the areas where his army operated and redistribute the sometimes thousands of acres to the peasants who had spent their lives toiling on it.

Villa was rather famous for leading an incursion into New Mexico, gaining him the enmity of the United States. General John J. Pershing tried to hunt down the bandit in Mexico in 1916. The United States was soon to enter into World War I, however, and the operation was called off without Villa ever being captured.

Villa would end up getting involved in politics only three years after he retired to an estate in 1920. He died in an assassination in 1923.

The Mexican Revolution had many other players involved, a multitude of ideologies and political ambitions behind its bloody battles and a mix of heroes and villains that make it an ideal period for Italian westerns. The oppression-fighting bandits and outlaws who sometimes rose to the level of national heroes only make the Mexican Revolution more romantic.

## European Politics and the Mexican Revolution

Zapata westerns were at the height of their popularity during the same period—1960s and 1970s—that spaghetti westerns were popular. These movies are very similar to other spaghetti westerns, at least on the outside. They oftentimes feature a lot of action and adventure, but quite a bit of character ambiguity. They're also, like other Italian westerns, not afraid to show how a character changes and is shaped by the events in the story.

The first in this line of movies is the Damiano Damiani film *A Bullet for the General*, featured later in this book. This film brings together characters that may seem like they don't belong in the same movie. We have the Mexican bandit, a slick American gangster and a government thug, two of those characters being wrapped up in one.

The aforementioned film shows the transformation of one of the lead characters from a rough, self-interested bandito into a genuine revolutionary who believes in the cause. According to Carlo Gaberscek, the writer of this particular film, Franco Solinas, was a very political sort and a Marxist writer. The theme of the peasants rising up and taking over a nation run by thugs, corrupt business interests and an exploitive bourgeois must have been enticing to such writers, and the results show in the films that they produced.

With these films, look for the revolutionary hero to emerge at some point in the story as a sort of role model. In some ways, these characters are actually more violent and complex incarnations of the singing cowboy. They stick up for the little people, they believe in something greater than themselves and they have a guiding sense of morality that, at least to some extent, dictates their actions.

Some of the films have simpler plots and celebrate the heroes of the Mexican Revolution in much the same way that American cowboy heroes—Wild Bill Hickok, for example—are celebrated in American film. *Seven for Pancho Villa*, for example, is a story that follows the famous revolutionary leader as he tries to get back gold that was stolen from him.

There is a lot to explore in this particular subgenre of spaghetti westerns. If you find yourself tiring of the same settings, taking a ride across the border and seeing what Mexico has to offer by way of adventure is certainly worth it. It's a nation that has a frontier history that is at once similar and very different than that of the U.S. The different political players involved, and the way that European writers viewed them, can make for some very entertaining cinema, to say the least, and some thoughtful material to mull over amidst a lot of violent, engaging and exciting action.

## The American Civil War

The American Civil War was over before the time period when most westerns take place. During the decades that most westerns are set in, the U.S. Army was at war with various Native American tribes, much of the manpower and firepower produced during the Civil War making its way westward and being used in a campaign of genocide and oppression that would become one of the most notorious and painful episodes in U.S. history.

The Civil War, however, does figure into some spaghetti westerns. It oftentimes provides an easy way to set up conflicts among characters, whether those conflicts will drive the story forward throughout the movie or whether they're just excuses to have the characters throw down in a gunfight.

*The Good, the Bad and the Ugly* does a great job of showing the futility of war and, in fact, some of the most emotional moments come during the scenes where Blondie and Tuco end up participating in a battle between Union and Confederate forces. Blondie and Tuco talk to a Union officer whose troops are enduring two bloody attacks a day over a bridge; it's something he can't see the sense in, but that he's bound by duty to endure.

Blondie asks him point blank why he doesn't just blow up the bridge and be done with it. The captain fantasizes about blowing it up, but both sides in the conflict have decided that the bridge has to be left intact and seized.

In this sequence, there's a great paradox. The violence in war, which is oftentimes shown in movies as something that makes the participants innately heroic, is shown as pointless, brutal and horrific. Blondie and Tuco don't see the point in it. They're killers, but they just don't see the point in all that killing for something so arbitrary as a bridge in the middle of nowhere. "I've never seen so many men wasted so badly," Blondie laments. Keep in mind that Blondie is a stone-cold killer, and he's shocked by the brutality of it all.

When Blondie and Tuco decide that blowing up the bridge would be great for their interests, it's easy enough to believe that they also do it out of some sense of wanting to end the slaughter. It's too late for the captain by the time that they do, but the captain does get the consolation of a bottle of liquor from Blondie and the sight of the two running off with dynamite to blow up the bridge, which they do in spectacular fashion. The captain doesn't make it, but Tuco and Blondie, in perhaps one of their most redeeming scenes, give him probably the thing he wanted most in life just before he expires.

## A Complex Concept of Violence

Anyone who watches these films already knows that violence is a lot more complex in these films than it is in most American westerns. There are few differences between the violence that protagonists and antagonists engage in and, even though the protagonists may engage in violence that's justified, it's still horrific. Where war is concerned, the rendering in these films can be equally thoughtful. Sometimes, you'll see the glory of a Mexican revolutionary riding into battle to protect their family, people and land from brutal oppressors. Sometimes you'll see young soldiers dying in a conflict that they don't understand in the loneliest and most painful ways possible. As was said, these are westerns for adults. There aren't always easy answers to every question or situation, and these films aren't afraid to address them appropriately.

## The Absence of Traditional Western Heroes

For viewers who like their westerns a bit more sophisticated than the norm, spaghetti westerns are ideal. These films eschew the types of heroes that people will be accustomed to from movie and television westerns popular through the '30s through '60s.

There are some exceptions to the Always Good trope used in some American westerns. *Shane*, for instance, features a rather brutal killing scene outside a saloon and the hero is a bit ambiguous in some regards. Where the Italians are concerned, however, the waters get even murkier.

Between the complex politics featured in these films and the expanded cast of characters, there is plenty to work with for the writers. They have Mexican banditos and soldiers, American frontier pioneers and scoundrels, crooked sheriffs and more. There is, essentially, so much going on in these movies that they don't suffer a bit from their lack of clear-cut good guys and bad guys. Get ready to cheer for the Natives in some of these films. Get ready to see Mexican outlaws that are every bit as clever and deadly as their American counterparts. The frontier in these films isn't a place where heroes battle villains and where civilization comes to tame the wilderness. It's a setting where people live and, as is the case with anything involving people, there is plenty of good, bad and ugly to go around. These films make it worth throwing off your preconceived notions of what a western should be and seeing what one really can be.

http://www.spaghetti-western.net/index.php/The_Spaghetti_Westerns_of_Sergio_Leone

http://realwestern.com/firearm/

http://spaghettiwesterns.1g.fi/guns.htm

http://www.questia.com/library/journal/1G1-245885444/zapata-westerns-the-short-life-of-a-subgenre-1966-1972

# Chapter 3

# Depth

Because of the ambiguous morality and the different perspective on the West, Italian westerns tend to have a lot more depth than some of their American counterparts. Not that there's anything wrong with Gene Autry and other honest-to-the-bone cowboys, but the films featuring those characters tend to be very tame and are almost always upholders of idealized morality. In Italian westerns, the characters, plots and the way that the films play out is usually much more complex and, in fact, realistic.

## Not the Average Western

What most Americans would think of as the white-hat, good-guy cowboy started to become a cultural fixture in the 1930s. Gene Autry is regarded as the first truly successful example of the singing cowboy, a paragon of virtue who rides into town with a white hat on a beautiful horse, charming everyone with a sincere smile. He's the ultimate good guy, basically.

This cowboy was the norm, though there were more vengeful examples, such as *The Lone Ranger*. Even in those cases, the violence was very tame and the good guys always won the day at the end. A delightful cowboy song usually wrapped up the action.

These are pleasant and fun myths and they're much loved, but one look at life in the real frontier would make it apparent that this was not the norm. The tropes in many American westerns are ones that are defined by simplicity and by romanticism. In some cases, an ugly shot of racism is added in as well.

The common trope in American westerns is that the hero, who is always good, has to defeat the villain, who is always bad. This can make for great fun, but the villains and heroes alike tend to have the depth of paper cutouts. The good guy is frequently a paladin-type character, sworn either by office of the law or personal philosophy to defend the weak, uphold the law and track down and bring the bad guys to justice. The villains are oftentimes defined by their schemes and little else.

In some of these westerns, the villain is presented as an exact opposite of the protagonist. This is oftentimes executed on-screen at a literal level, with the bad guy wearing a black hat to contrast with the good guy's white hat. In fact, this is so established that white-hat and black-hat are still used as euphemisms for good and bad in modern life.

None of this is to say that the American westerns are bad films. Quite the contrary. Some of them are excellent films. Films such as *The Big Country* are examples of good westerns that, more or less, tend to follow the good vs. bad concept. In Hollywood westerns—at least the ones that preceded the spaghetti western craze—it's never so much a question of whether the good guys will win, but it's rather a question of when and how the good guys are going to win. In spaghetti westerns, there's oftentimes not even a good guy to root for.

## Gunfights

While the differences in plots and characters might be markedly different between Hollywood westerns and spaghetti westerns, the nature of the actual combat is oftentimes very similar. The violence in spaghetti westerns may be more graphic and visceral than it is in most Hollywood westerns that came before, but the abilities of the heroes are oftentimes quite similar.

In spaghetti westerns, the hero is often possessed of abilities with a pistol that go beyond both the capabilities of human beings and the capabilities of firearms of the time. The weapons fire with the accuracy, deadliness and reliability of modern firearms. They are fired by men whose abilities are far beyond human.

The Man with No Name is a particularly good example of this. He can gun down several opponents without even raising his barrel to eye level—which is the way that one actually aims a gun with such precision—while fanning the hammer to enable rapid fire and somehow never getting hit—or almost never—by his opponent's bullets. In essence, the hero's six-shooter oftentimes performs like a modern machine gun while the antagonists have firearms that perform the way one might expect a pistol from the 19th century to behave: slow, inaccurate and not particularly reliable.

Here's an example taken from the modern day. According to the New York Times, reporting in 2007, New York City police fired 472 times in 2005. They hit 82 times out of those 472 shots, bringing their percentage rate of hits to 17.4 percent. These are trained police officers firing modern firearms that are accurate, reliable and with which they are very thoroughly trained.

Compare that to the Man with No Name in the beginning of *A Fistful of Dollars*. He hits four bad guys with four shots, for a 100 percent hit rate, sustaining no injuries and not running for cover. The bad guys fire a lot, with a zero percent hit rate while creating a crossfire pattern, judging by how they're positioned. Simply put, just as can be said of the gunfighters in early Hollywood westerns, no one is that good.

This happens repeatedly in these films. The men who carry their six-shooters low on their hip are fast beyond belief. They are accurate beyond the capabilities of their firearms and they oftentimes manage to squeeze far more than six shots out of their six-shot cylinder. The logistics aren't really where the myths exist in these films, however, or, at least, not the important part. Those gunfighters—Blondie, Tuco, Navajo Joe—they're myths through and through.

## Real Violence in the Old West

Where spaghetti westerns oftentimes succeed is in showing that violence is graphic, the consequences are oftentimes permanent and that the innocent are often the ones gunned down. Where it plays into myths is in portraying some men as supernaturally able to survive gunfight after gunfight and being more than willing to throw down in a duel on the main street of a dusty town.

In reality, this type of violence was generally viewed on the frontier with much the same shock and dismay that it is viewed with in today's world. "Gunfighter" is a rather recent term and it wasn't used in the Old West. If you shot someone down in a saloon over cards, you were a gambler and a murderer. People who had deadly reputations oftentimes went out of their way to avoid fights. After all, if someone else has a reputation as a particularly deadly type, you don't do well at staying alive by seeking them out and challenging them to a duel. Add to this that medical technology was nowhere near where it is today and even a seemingly minor bullet injury could fester and kill, often painfully and over an agonizing amount of time. One film that does do this well is *Once Upon a Time in the Old West* where one of the most likeable characters ends up dying from a gut wound that's been getting worse for days.

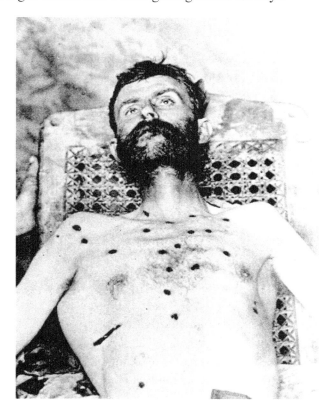

Violence in the Old West was just as terrifying as it is today. Gunfights were chaotic, random and oftentimes erupted when people were drunk and gambling. Killing enough men to become a master of it was as likely to land one in prison or get one executed as it is today.

## Faster Than You'll Ever Live to Be

Here's a scenario people who have seen most any western will know very well. Two men, both equally deadly, meet on an abandoned street. They both wear their pistols low on their hips. They stare one another down as the townsfolk hide behind swinging doors, grimy windows, barrels and crates. The men size one another up, both predators, both committed to a game where the loser will lose everything and the winner will be the one who walks away.

They stare. The sun beats down. They sweat. Finally, one of them goes for his gun. He's a quarter-second too slow or a few inches too inaccurate, however, and the hero puts a round in his chest before the villain, who almost always draws first, can react. The villain is cut down and the hero walks away. Perhaps he twirls his gun before he holsters it, hops on his horse and rides into the sunset.

This is a Hollywood invention that became a staple of western films. Variations on it include shootout at the O.K. Corral, which was an actual shootout, but which has been replayed over and over in films with a lot of mythology on top of it. Here's the reality.

First, the hero and villain both ride into town, guns hanging from their hips. This doesn't really jibe with the reality of the Old West.

In 1882, a Texas cattle-raising association had already banned cowboys from carrying revolvers. This is *Texas*, one of the states more associated with gunfighter mythology than any other. How about Tombstone, Arizona? The town's name alone implies that one better ride in packing a lot of firepower. That would have gotten you fined. Firearms were certainly a part of the American West, but those who were carrying them were required to check them with the sheriff before they rode into Tombstone. In Arizona today, gun laws are looser than they were during the time of Wyatt Earp.

Even some of the most notorious Old West towns, including Deadwood, South Dakota, had very strict gun laws. There was a lot of public sentiment at the time against carrying guns in cities. It was easy to see why someone would want one if they were riding out in the wilderness, but having one in town was something that was widely regarded as a problem to be dealt with.

Need to get the hell out of Dodge? Be sure to stop at the sheriff's office and pick up your gun first, because you're not going to be carrying it around with you at the saloon.

When gunfights did erupt, they weren't so noble or duel-like as one would expect today. Gunfighters—even that is a Hollywood term, more than anything—were not stupid. If they wanted to off someone, they usually waited for the right time and ambushed them. This is actually played straight in *The Unforgiven*, where the violence is oftentimes brutal and realistic.

Truth be told, only a fool would stand in front of someone and see who could shoot faster. This did happen, of course, but dueling had already become looked upon as savage, unnecessary and criminal long before the Old West was being settled by the U.S. Even founders such as Franklin openly criticized the practice. Several Western states, including such popular cowboy stomping grounds as Nevada, New Mexico, Colorado, Idaho and Oklahoma, have prohibitions on dueling written right into the law.

In the real Old West, fighting the bad guy on the main street with a pistol in an arranged duel would not have been looked upon as noble, in all likelihood. The winner would not have ridden away, triumphant, into the sunset. He likely would have been facing a murder charge.

The reality of gun violence in the Old West, according to many sources, was much like the reality of gun violence today. It usually represented an escalation over a petty argument—card games, etc.—involved more misses than hits and wound up with someone going to jail, and possibly people who weren't even involved in the dispute losing their lives.

## They're Samurai

*A Fistful of Dollars* is actually not a particularly original film. The film company Toho, out of Japan, actually managed to win a lawsuit based on this film being a remake of *Yojimbo*, a 1961 samurai flick by Kurosawa. In many regards, the characters in these films do behave like samurai or other ancient warriors.

These characters oftentimes have vendettas based on honor or based on vengeance, or both. They seek to have it out with the offending party. The sequence in *Once Upon a Time in the West* where Harmonica saves Frank from being assassinated is particularly good as an example of this. He doesn't save Frank because he wants Frank to live; Harmonica saves Frank because Harmonica wants to be the one to put a bullet in Frank.

This makes for wonderful entertainment, but it is largely fictionalized. People have always been people. People do not seek out ways to get themselves killed in the course of seeking revenge, unless they are truly deranged. In reality, Blondie and Tuco probably would have shot Angel Eyes and then one another, or Tuco would have just shot Blondie while he was asleep, rode up to Sad Hill and gotten ambushed by Angel Eyes before he even knew the mercenary was there.

Why the historical inaccuracies? Because spaghetti westerns and westerns in general are about myths and legends and that's largely what makes them so enjoyable. People as fast and deadly as Harmonica, Django and Blondie probably never existed, and their real-life counterparts—such as Billy the Kid—were really, really bad guys, but it's nice to think that they did, in the same way that it's nice to think that Aragorn could kill 30 orcs without breaking a sweat.

## Still Waters Run Deep

What about those tormented souls who ride the endless expanses of the West, looking for revenge, money or whatever else the movie has them after? What are they underneath? This is where spaghetti westerns really shine. While singing cowboys can be a lot of fun, they lack a certain humanity. No one is that good and, if they were, they'd probably be working for charity rather than chasing cows around and getting into gunfights. The protagonists in spaghetti westerns are usually complex characters, even if they're involved in rather simple stories.

Ryan from *Death Rides a Horse* keeps his cards close to his chest. He's not telling people that he's going to be their hero and, in fact, he doesn't let on as to what he knows about Bill's own quest for vengeance, or how he's tied up in it as well.

The Man with No Name is oftentimes the Man with Nothing to Say, as well. He doesn't let on as to what he knows, what he's planning or how he intends for it to all turn out, just like someone in his line of work would likely do. He's a schemer, a plotter and a master criminal and he keeps things under wraps as much as possible, not even letting poor Tuco know that he has no intention of letting him hang.

Harmonica doesn't let anyone know what he's up to, even the man he wants to kill. He plays mournful notes on a harmonica—hence the name—but *Once Upon a Time in the West* isn't afraid to introduce this murky hero and let him play out his story without making everything clear. In the end, it's easy to sympathize with him, as he was put through a horrible trauma as a child by the man he wants to kill. The revelation, however, makes Harmonica seem even more like a ghost. A remnant of a once-living person damned to replay the same horrible event over and over until he completes a task and is set free. Finally freed, he wanders off with another dead friend who, until the end of the film, was starting to seem like someone who could have been genuine family to Harmonica.

In some cases, strength and intelligence are implied by the silence of the characters. Ramon in *A Fistful of Dollars* goes on and on about how to kill a man. The Man with No Name isn't nearly as verbal, but he remembers everything and exploits the weakness that Ramon demonstrates in revealing too much about himself.

Tuco, who is no buffoon but who is also no steam-engine scientist, babbles a lot in *The Good, the Bad and the Ugly*. Oftentimes, what he says reveals that he's not quite as smart as Blondie. This is particularly striking in the "It's for you" scene where Tuco can't read a note addressed to "idiots"; Blondie calmly reads it and makes a witty remark, revealing his intelligence.

In spaghetti westerns, look for protagonists who take a long time to let you know what they're really up to. Generally speaking, the less they say, the more is going on in their heads and, oftentimes, their plans are so complex that verbalizing them would be tedious, but watching them unfold is glorious.

## Influences: From Warriors to Peasants

These characters oftentimes represent archetypes. McBain and his family in *Once Upon a Time in the Old West*, for instance, are the archetypical pioneer family. McBain bought some land—and made a very good move, in that regard—and has a dream to make a good life for himself and his family. He's come to the West seeking fortune and prosperity, not guns and violence.

In *A Bullet for the General*, we get to see the character who goes from being a true bad guy to someone who has something to believe in. He is the reformed crook, an archetypical character that can be very engaging on-screen.

In *Navajo Joe*, we have the true warrior. He's on a righteous mission and he's not going to fail, even if it means his life. One of the things that make this movie interesting is that Joe manages to be a three-dimensional character. Without making him into a noble savage stereotype, the movie allows him to develop into a true force for vengeance and it's thrilling to watch, just as it is to watch any other warrior in a film.

There are plenty of reinventions of stock characters in these films, but the Italian filmmakers did them one better and raised the bar for developing them. They may not be singing cowboys but, as Cheyenne's conversation with Harmonica in the roadhouse established, some people make music with guns. What tune they're playing often establishes what type of character they really are. Quite often, they turn out to be clever variations on archetypes, whether they're the reformed prostitute with the heart of gold, the gunslinger who has an epiphany and realized there's more to life and murder and mayhem or the cold-blood killer who surprises the audience with a moment of genuine compassion.

One thoroughly enjoyable subset of spaghetti westerns are the Zapata westerns, those that center on the Mexican revolutions. For American audiences who haven't seen these, they're a fresh way to look at the mythology of the West with a new group of heroes and villains and, quite often, the stakes for which both are fighting are much higher. They're not fighting over railroad rights or a coffin full of gold; they're fighting for the future of a nation and a people and these films are not to be missed.

## Enjoying the Depth

When you watch the films in the upcoming chapters, look for a lot of symbolism. Look for a lot of information being revealed by what is not said or what is just implied rather than for long expositions. These films can sometimes be hard to follow because of the tendency to use silence and symbolism so readily on the part of the directors, but they're also excellent in that they give the audience more to think about.

The characters in these films oftentimes do fit archetypes, and Western tropes common across the entire genre—American and Italian—are seen in these films, but that doesn't detract from what they have to offer. In fact, it makes them more interesting in many regards, and very memorable, as well.

http://www.nytimes.com/2007/12/09/weekinreview/09baker.html?pa gewanted=all&_r=0

http://books.google.com/books?id=pbLA3HzgjW8C&pg=PA316&d q=yodeling+cowboy++tradition&hl=en&ei=ow9uTrW4LoPi0QGcg-XlBA&sa=X&oi=book_result&ct=book-preview-link&resnum=1&ved=0CDYQuwUwAA#v=onepage&q=yodeling%20cowboy%20%20tradition&f=false

http://www.filmsite.org/westernfilms.html

http://twrpcactusrose.blogspot.com/2009/06/old-west-gunfighter-reality-or-myth.html

http://www.ndsu.edu/pubweb/~rcollins/scholarship/guns.html

http://latinamericanhistory.about.com/od/thehistoryofmexico/a/mexi canrevo.htm

# Chapter 4

# The Music and Sound

A huge part of the appeal of spaghetti westerns is the music. They have their own distinctive style of music, with Ennio Morricone being the real trendsetter as far as how these movies sound. They're oftentimes eclectic in terms of the instrumentation and, quite often, they use sounds in them that diverge significantly from the orchestral instruments that dominated, and still dominate, most movie soundtracks.

## Ennio Morricone

There's no one quite as strongly associated with the sound of spaghetti westerns as is Ennio Morricone. He's still alive and well—and working—well into his 80s. He has worked with pop music artists, conducted orchestras and has composed in excess of a hundred classical pieces during his lifetime. He also redefined the western soundtrack, and is as much associated with spaghetti westerns as are directors such as Leone.

While this man is associated with spaghetti westerns, one fails to understand his importance to film music in general if they only see him as the man who gave the Man with No Name a rousing score to accompany his on-screen feats. Morricone has also scored films including *Cinema Paradiso, The Thing, Bulworth* and many others. He is a respected conductor, trumpet player and more.

If you love the theme from *The Good, the Bad and the Ugly,* you're not alone. A version of this film recorded by Hugo Montenegro sold in excess of 1 million copies. The first bars of this piece, usually played on a flute, is one of the most distinctive leitmotivs in modern music, film or otherwise.

*The Ecstasy of Gold,* used during the Sad Hill Cemetery sequence in *The Good, the Bad and the Ugly* has been used by rock bands, rappers and beyond in various ways and is one of the most distinctive western soundtrack pieces in the world.

## What to Listen For

On any Morricone soundtrack, listen for a particularly eclectic collection of instruments. Muted trumpets, flutes, and other orchestral instruments are sometimes accompanied by electric guitars and other more modern instruments, adding a wonderfully thrilling effect. In some instances, simple 4/4 ostinato drumming will invoke Native American themes, while wailing trumpets may invoke Mexico in others. His work on *Navajo Joe* is particularly notable, though not as well noticed as his work in other films. A wild, discordant and really quite disturbing play on Native American singing opens up the theme before it soars into an electric guitar-driven, dark and tense theme, with drums coming in frequently to reference the origins of the hero.

Morricone also understood how to do eerie very well. *Once Upon a Time in the West* has some very abstract sound in it, sometimes executed so well that it sounds like part of the ambient sound in the scene, but nevertheless lending a very haunting quality. Morricone could raise music to the heights of triumphalism without being bombastic and he could be so subtle as to make the soundtrack barely noticeable. He could give a character more personality by assigning to them just the right musical representation, he could make a wide shot of the desert seem even more empty than what was represented on the screen and he sometimes threw in jolting sounds that made for some very well-executed moments of tension in these films. A pipe organ that pops up in *For a Few Dollars More* is particularly jarring, but entirely appropriate for the scene in which it is the most prominent.

More than anything, listen for creativity in these soundtracks, as that's what Morricone really lends to the films. His success in scoring films goes far beyond his ability to translate his music into significant record sales and to no small extent he did define the way that these movies sound.

## Other Great Soundtracks

Many of these films have memorable soundtracks. The main theme from *Django*, sung by Rocky Roberts and composed by Luis Bacalov has a wonderful lounge-music feel to it and manages, somehow, to be very good without being cheesy, even though it seems to try its hardest to be the latter at times.

*A Bullet for the General* has a great soundtrack as well, celebrating the film's Mexican setting without resorting to cliché.

For a lampshade of this, *The Outlaw Jose Wales*, not a spaghetti western but one that features their most notable star, has a scene where two women Wales rescues start singing awfully, accompanied by equally awful instrumentation courtesy of a concertina, sending a dog into a fit of howling.

## Patience

In these films, one is likely to get no small amount of instruction in patience. Leone's films are famous—some might even say notorious—for this. The man was not afraid to burn a lot of frames of film on someone standing there staring at their rival. Sound oftentimes plays a big part in setting up the tension.

It might be a breeze, the creaking of a windmill or anything else, but these films tend to involve the viewer with the sounds of the scene as much as they do with the action.

There are some aural deficiencies that the modern viewer will likely hear in these films. For instance, it's not uncommon to hear the exact same gunshot or ricochet sound over and over again in the same film, or even between several different films. This might be distracting but it doesn't take away from the action too much and, certainly, those same flaws are to be found in modern movies, except the bass is usually much more pronounced and the clarity better.

Perhaps one of the best uses of sound is in the opening sequences of *Once Upon a Time in the West.* In this sequence—detailed in the entry on this film—the absence of natural sounds clues one of the characters into the fact that something is amiss. In fact, it's the definition of the clichéd line, "It's quiet; too quiet," but it's executed in a way that is anything but clichéd.

Low-budget films have to make the most of what they have on hand. For storytelling purposes, sound is used in these films heavily. Be aware, however, that it's sometimes the absence of sound that tells a story. This might take some getting used to, but there are few things in this world that make people as nervous as silence and spaghetti westerns aren't afraid to capitalize on that, particularly if they're Leone's work.

## Sound and Tension Tropes

There is some fun to be had in the way that sound is handled in these films. Some of the use of sound is brilliant, and some of it has the same flaws that you'll find in any other film, Italian or otherwise, of any era. They don't necessarily detract from the film, but there are some truly unrealistic elements to these films where sound is concerned.

## Pull the Hammer Back

This trope exists in just about every film that involves a gun at some point. It's not a flaw and, in fact, what's being portrayed when this trope is used is one of the most intimidating scenarios imaginable. Someone sticks a gun in someone's face and, at some point, they pull the hammer back to let whoever's staring down the barrel know that the gunman is serious.

TV Tropes calls this the Dramatic Gun Cock and there's really no more suitable term for it. Guns are nearly characters in some westerns and, when they're not, they're usually extensions of a character, at the very least.

Because some people love to be specific about guns in movies, there are some redeeming qualities in these westerns that deserve to be mentioned.

Unless the time is in the 20th century or soon before, most of the handguns in use will be single-action revolvers. On such a gun, pulling back the hammer rotates a fresh round—if one is loaded—in front of the hammer and prepares the firing pin to strike the primer. In a cap-and-ball revolver, the action is largely the same, excepting that a percussion cap is struck when the hammer falls rather than the primer on a cartridge round. For each time these revolvers are fired, the hammer must be manually pulled back and cocked again to rotate the cylinder and prepare the weapon to fire.

In modern movies, you'll hear a very similar clicking noise to that which a single-action revolver makes at entirely inappropriate times. For example, the person holding the gun might pull the hammer back on a semi-automatic pistol—some have them—and then pull it back again, without firing, which is a completely redundant action. It would require the gun holder to lower the hammer and click it again, apparently wanting to juice as much intimidation as they can out of that gun without actually firing it.

A single-action is a bit different. The click-click noise would, in fact, come in advance of any shot that was fired, making repeated uses of this sound entirely realistic. If the hero were to fire four rounds out of their Peacemaker, they could realistically threaten a disarmed or wounded baddie with a cocked hammer. This would not work on a modern semi-automatic, as a round would be loaded into the chamber as soon as the last one was expelled, hence the term "automatic" being part of the name.

The click-click noise can be used for great effect. Oftentimes, it translates to "This is your last chance," "I'm savoring this" or "I'm dead serious." In scenes where someone is getting ambushed, the ambusher will oftentimes announce that they're in the room by cocking the hammer back before they announce themselves. Their gun does the talking.

Before someone tries to say that cocking a gun repeatedly is unnecessary and a mark of bad filmmaking, realize that, in the era of single-action revolvers, this was necessary and the dramatic use of it is entirely warranted, and very effective.

## Gunfire Galore
Whenever a gunfight breaks out in films, the sound is as much a part of the action as the actual bullets. In spaghetti westerns, it sometimes becomes nearly ridiculous with the amount of gunfire going on, but it adds to the action. If you want to get technical about it, however, there are some technical glitches that exist just for the sake of storytelling.

Many of the characters in these movies are soft-spoken killers who spend a lot of their lives gunning down their rivals. In reality, most of them would be anything but soft-spoken. They would have been shouting just to hear themselves.

The characters in these films are oftentimes shooing large-caliber handguns and rifles repeatedly, and having quiet conversations right thereafter. This is not quite realistic. When a gun goes off, the shooter is instantly exposed to a very loud percussive pop. It's much louder than is represented in most films—averaging around 140 decibels, far over the threshold for painful noises—and, in the case of some firearms, it's not so much a booming noise as it is a very hard popping noise. This causes temporary deafness, which is usually not total, but which diminishes the ability to hear significantly. A loud ringing in the ears usually immediately follows a gunshot.

The reason for this is that the body does have a reflex that protects the ears from sustained barrages of loud noise, but it cannot protect against the sort of percussive pops that occur in a fraction of a second that characterize the sound of gunfire. Each shot does the same damage and that damage is cumulative.

Anyone who has done a lot of shooting without ear protection has lost a good portion of their hearing. It's inevitable; it's just physiology. No matter how much someone may fit the bill as a hardened killer, their ears are still as tender as anyone else's and they will take damage from the shots fired, each and every time.

In scenes where even larger and faster-firing guns are being used, such as Gatling guns, the damage would be worse. Those guns are just as loud or louder than the other firearms used in these movies. If cannons are being used, the noise would be absolutely deafening. Most cannon crews would turn their backs and plug their ears when firing, and they'd still suffer hearing loss.

The gunplay in these movies is a bit more realistic than it is in most American westerns, but realize that it's still a fantasy in some regards. The sound of gunfire is traumatic to the ears, muzzle flashes are blinding in some cases and the black powder used in guns during the times when some of these films were set left a thick, black cloud of smoke in its wake. The first shot may have been dead-on accurate, but the second would have had to have been made through that cloud of smoke.

For a more realistic idea of what gunfire—a lot of gunfire, in particular—is like, see the opening sequences of *Saving Private Ryan*. It might be set a century after the time in which some spaghetti westerns take place, but the shots back in the frontier days were loud as well, and the disorientation, ringing in the ears and eventual deafness would be inevitable results of being a gunslinger who shot too much.

## Appreciating the Sound

It's easy to pick out flaws. In low-budget movies, it's really like shooting fish in a barrel. Where these movies really succeed, however, is in being engaging despite their flaws. The gunfire might consist of a few repeated sounds, but the plot and the way that it makes the viewer engage with the character makes the gunfire sound just as deadly as it needs to be, and it won't be long before you forget about hearing the same ricochet noise over and over.

In some ways, these spaghetti westerns are actually far superior to westerns that had much higher budgets, and this is apparent in the soundtracks. These soundtracks took the cowboy archetype and give it an entirely new aural dimension. The soundtracks, like the films, are much darker and edgier than the soundtracks that you'll see in most Hollywood films. When someone is whistling in the soundtrack, it's not the sort of happy whistling someone might do when they're riding the range; it's usually very eerie. When Native American music is referenced, it's oftentimes haunting and heroic, rather than simply being used as another way to stereotype Native Americans.

These films have a powerful sound dimension to them that often suits the music. Several sources mention that one of the reasons that Leone drew some scenes out for so long is that he wanted the audience to hear the music. He was right, in this regard, as there wouldn't be any Man with No Name without Morricone's score, Harmonica wouldn't be as haunting a character without his namesake instrument and Navajo Joe was a certified badass who deserved a theme that referenced where he came from.

For the other things that spaghetti westerns have to offer, the soundtracks are oftentimes among the most memorable and, if you grew up watching these films, hearing one of them, even without seeing the movie, will many times bring up some great memories.

The soundtracking style of these movies endured as well. Tarantino oftentimes uses music that seems not at all to fit the scene, just as these movies brought in growling electric guitars to announce arrival of a true threat, even though these movies often take place more than a hundred years before electric guitars even existed.

As was said, crank the sound when you watch these movies. Their low-budget limitations don't hold them back. In fact, those limitations often resulted in some of the most creative uses of sound you'll hear in any films and, occasionally, very creative uses of no sound at all.

http://tvtropes.org/pmwiki/pmwiki.php/Main/DramaticGunCock

# Chapter 5

# The Essential and Memorable Actors and Actresses

As is the case with any other film genre, there are certain actors who are very much associated with spaghetti westerns. Because of the international casts in these films, some of these actors will be more familiar to people who are from specific nations than others. A few of them had longstanding careers before they started acting in spaghetti westerns, and for others, their careers really took off after they started appearing in these films.

Many spaghetti westerns are dubbed, so the voices of some of the actors and actresses you hear on the screen are not their actual voices. Of course, in many of these movies, some of the characters hardly speak at all, which had to be convenient, to say the least.

Here are some of the names associated with spaghetti westerns. Among them, you'll find some actors who got opportunities to play against the usual type of characters that they portrayed in films, allowing them to expand their repertoires to include some memorable, and unexpected, roles.

## Clint Eastwood

There's probably no American actor more associated with the spaghetti western genre than Clint Eastwood. Eastwood, born in 1930, got his first big break in the western genre on television, playing a supporting character in the series *Rawhide*, a conventional but beloved TV western. It was in Italian westerns that the image of Clint Eastwood that persists today would be forged.

Eastwood is most famous for playing the Man with No Name, possibly the single most famous character from all spaghetti westerns. His trademark squint, ability to play a very emotionally distant but compelling character and physical presence made him an ideal antihero character. It also allowed him to get away from the image that his work on *Rawhide* gave him, making him edgier, darker and more dangerous.

Eastwood became popular in Italy following his debut in *A Fistful of Dollars*. At the time that the film was made, Eastwood and director Sergio Leone were not well-known names, but following the creation of the Man with No Name, both would become legendary.

Eastwood's career continued to thrive after his spaghetti western roles, and continues to do so today. He's directed and appeared in what are regarded as some of the best American westerns, including *The Outlaw Jose Wales* and *The Unforgiven*. While the height of spaghetti westerns may be decades in the past, Eastwood's characters, particularly in westerns, still have elements of the Man with No Name in them. His hard stare, fast draw and loner nature continued to be parts of his character in westerns that followed the Italian pictures where he made his mark.

Eastwood has become a cultural icon outside of his western films. Characters such as Dirty Harry—a tough, abrasive cop—for instance, are just as famous and popular as his western characters.

## Henry Fonda

Henry Fonda (1905-1982) is a legendary American actor whose roles included a diverse range of characters. He performed in everything from Broadway productions to comedies to intense and well-regarded dramas. Fonda was a native of Nebraska, the son of an advertising printer.

Fonda's career started early in the 20th century, with his first film role being in the 1935 film *The Farmer Takes a Wife*. He appeared in a slew of films over the following decades, including westerns such as *The Return of Frank James*. He served in the Navy during World War II and reached the level of Lieutenant Junior Grade. He was awarded the Navy Presidential Unit Citation and The Bronze Star.

His roles in westerns during the 1960s included *How the West Was Won*. Sergio Leone wanted him for the role of Frank, the Big Bad in *Once Upon a Time in the West*, but Fonda initially turned it down. Finally convinced to take the role, he ended up turning in a performance that is, without a doubt, one of the best in spaghetti westerns.

Playing strongly against type, Fonda portrays a ruthless killer and bandit who is making at least an attempt—if not succeeding—at becoming a more legitimate businessman. His sadistic nature and habit of settling everything with a revolver—something which Frank is terrifyingly good at—make him into the villain in the film, however, and the subject of a longstanding grudge held by the main character.

While he wasn't a regular cast member in spaghetti westerns, Frank is certainly a character who epitomizes the bad guys in these films: tough, ruthless, heartless and deadly.

## Lee Van Cleef

Lee Van Cleef, Jr (1925-1989) was widely known for his western roles. He was also a character actor, oftentimes taking the role of a villain or, at least, as a hero who was morally ambiguous.

Van Cleef appeared in American westerns including *The Man Who Shot Liberty Valance* and *High Noon*. His work was

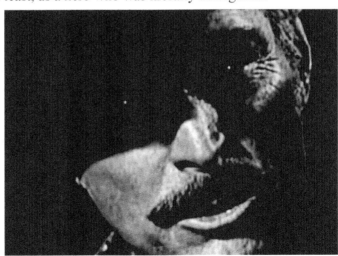

very much associated with the western genre, but started to degrade during the late 1950s. He saw his career get back on track with ihs appearance in *For a Few Dollars More*, playing a protagonist in that film. Sergio Leone chose to cast him again in the third installment of the Man with No Name Trilogy, this time as Angel Eyes in *The Good, the Bad and the Ugly*, allowing Van Cleef to portray one of the most frightening and cold-blooded villains in any of these films.

Van Cleef, as seen in the image above, had a very sharp nose, hard eyes and could affect an intimidating visage. His role as Angel Eyes allowed him to work with a character who was sharp, ruthless and just as deadly as the Man with No Name, but even more removed from the people around him. He was missing the tip of one of the fingers on his right hand, the result of a carpentry accident, which can be clearly seen in the final showdown sequence in *The Good, the Bad and the Ugly*. If anything, it lends more realism to this mercenary character that has certainly seen his share of fights.

He did a lot of work in the spaghetti western genre, sometimes as a hero and sometimes as a villain. He appears in such films as *Death Rides a Horse*—featured late in this book—and *Day of Anger*.

Van Cleef continued to act into the 1980s, appearing in television shows, including a brief stint playing a ninja warrior in the early '80s series *The Master*. *The Master* was not widely regarded as a good series, even being featured on the satire show *Mystery Science Theater 3000*. Van Cleef, however, enjoyed a career that lasted nearly 40 years and is one of the most prominent American actors in the spaghetti western genre.

## Eli Wallach

Eli Wallach, currently 98 years old and still going, had a career that spanned from 1945 to 2010. He was a military officer during World War II, and studied alongside actors including Brando and Clift. He appeared in a wide range of films, not surprising given the incredible length of his acting career.

His most famous spaghetti western role is as Tuco in *The Good, the Bad and the Ugly*. Not Mexican himself, Wallach portrayed Mexican bandit Tuco in a way that allowed the character to define himself rather than as a sidekick to his "frenemy" Blondie, aka the Man with No Name.

The character is one of the most notable and well known among the huge cast of anti-heroes and villains that appear in spaghetti westerns. The performance, while Wallach was chosen because he did have a lot of natural ability to be comical, was one where the buffoonish actions of the character were offset by moments where the audience is reminded that Tuco is not to be trifled with and is, most certainly, one of the deadliest men in the room, no matter who else might be standing in the room with him.

According to multiple sources, Sergio Leone and Wallach had a good relationship with one another until a contractual obligation forced Leone to choose actor Rod Steiger for a role that he had convinced Wallach to take, at the expense of another job for Wallach. Wallach was furious about the incident, even though there was little Leone could do about it and Wallach was Leone's first choice.

Wallach continued to perform in film and television productions until he retired in 2010. His reputation extends far beyond the realm of spaghetti westerns, but his portrayal of Tuco is still one of his most remarkable and memorable appearances. He also convinced Henry Fonda to take the role of Frank in *Once Upon a Time in the West*, contributing to the creation of yet another very memorable—and frightening—Old West outlaw in Italian westerns.

## Jack Palance

Jack Palance had a reputation for playing rugged, tough characters and it wasn't just acting skill behind his effectiveness in those roles. He was a former professional boxer, Air Force veteran and all-around tough guy who could still manage to be funny, engaging and very witty. He had a distinctive look and there were plenty of stories about how it came to be, mostly involving one heroic action or another, such as a well-known story about him having to bail out of a flaming bomber during World War II. According to Palance, such stories were just the work of Hollywood press agents.

Palance appears in spaghetti westerns including *Chato's Land*, where he plays a villain. He also appears in *Welcome to Blood City* and *The Desperados*. His intimidating countenance, pictured above, makes him an ideal actor for these films. His comedic talents were put on display in the film *City Slickers*, for which he won an Academy Award.

Palance was also a musician, having released a country album during the 1960s.

## Charles Bronson

Charles Bronson (1921-2003) was a decorated World War II veteran. He came from very humble roots, the son of a coal miner, and didn't learn to speak English until his teens, though he was born in Pennsylvania.

Bronson started his acting career on stage in Philadelphia. He relocated to Hollywood in 1950 and appeared in several films as in minor roles. He played alongside horror legend Vincent Price in *House of Wax*, though he had no lines, as the character he played was mute.

His real success came in the 1960s, with some of his most prominent roles being in westerns such as *The Magnificent Seven*. He also played soldiers, prisoners of war and various western characters.

In the late 1960s, he started acting in spaghetti westerns. He appeared most famously as the character Harmonica, pictured above, in Leone's epic *Once Upon a Time in the West*. He was known as a loner in real life and, on-screen, he demonstrated that personality to great effect in portraying this character. He had actually turned down the role of Angel Eyes in *The Good, the Bad and the Ugly* and the lead in *A Fistful of Dollars*.

He also appeared in *Chato's Land*, along with Jack Palance. Other roles include *Bataille de San, Soleil Rouge* and many others.

Bronson's foray into Italian westerns went along well with his tough, rugged image. He would later become a modern-day vigilante in the *Death Wish* series of films and is well known as a familiar face in many World War II action films.

He retired in 1998 as the result of medical issues. He died of pneumonia and suffered from Alzheimer's disease in his later years.

## Giuliano Gemma (Montgomery Wood)

Giuliano Gemma (1938-2013) had a background as a stuntman before he started as a full-fledged actor. He appeared in an array of

famous spaghetti westerns, including *Blood for a Silver Dollar, Day of Anger* and *A Pistol for Ringo*, with that last film listed later in the book.

He ended up having a long career as an actor, spanning until 2013, when he died at the age of 75. He even starred in a web comic. His death, despite his advanced age, came prematurely. He was killed in a car accident in Italy and died after being brought to the hospital. He is sometimes listed in credits as Montgomery Wood.

## Klaus Kinsky

Klaus Kinsky (1926-1991) was a very respected actor who started out in theatre. He entered the world of film in the late 1940s, after having served in the German army during World War II. The actor was injured and captured by the British while fighting in the Netherlands. Kinsky claimed to have deserted on purpose, wanting to get out of the German army. His captivity extended for two years after the war, when he was finally allowed to return home.

While he was a respected actor, he also appeared in many exploitation films. His spaghetti western roles include *A Bullet for the General, For a Few Dollars More* and *The Great Silence.*

Kinsky had a reputation as an explosive person and a womanizer. According to some sources, this was largely exaggerated, sometimes by the actor himself. Throughout his career, he did not shy away from films as controversial as his personality, including *Aguirre, The Wrath of God*, a 1972 picture about a conquistador trying to make his way down the Amazon that was renowned for its violence and for its unique production style.

## Marianne Koch

Marianne Koch is a German actress. She no longer performs, but appeared in several spaghetti westerns, earning her a place among the established actresses of this genre.

Koch was featured in *A Fistful of Dollars*, making her one of the prominent characters in one of the most famous westerns out of Italy. She had a very active career during the 1950s-1970s, appearing in nearly seventy films in a range of different genres. She currently holds an MD and worked as a practicing physician until the late 1990s. She has also appeared on numerous German television shows, for which she has been presented awards and enjoys widespread recognition in that nation.

## Ida Galli

Unlike many spaghetti western cast members, Ida Galli (1959-1990) is primarily known for her roles in these films. She also worked under the names Isli Oberon, Arianna and Evelyn Stewart.

Galli's better-known spaghetti western appearances include the films *La coda dello scorpione, Il coltello di ghiaccio* and *Sette note in nero.*

Her work continued up until her untimely death in 1990. She credited much of her success to being a genre actress and to using the more American name Evelyn Stewart, which she used up until her last films.

## Erika Blanc

Erika Blanc—real name Enrica Bianchi Colombatto—is as well known for her roles in horror films as she is for her work in spaghetti westerns. The actress appeared in some truly off-the-wall spaghetti westerns, including *El karate, el Colt y el impostor*, a film that brought together martial-arts action with cowboy-gun-fighting mayhem.

Blanc continues to work today, having appeared in television movies, mini-series and films, as well as shorts. She has over a hundred filmography credits on IMDb as of 2014 and is still going strong.

## Nicoletta Machiavelli

Machiavelli is, in fact, a descendant of the most famous person to bear that name, the author of *The Prince* and the namesake for a particularly cold type of manipulation. This actress, however, is notable for her appearances in many spaghetti westerns, including some of the most notable films and franchises.

She appeared in *A Noose for Django*, featuring one of the most popular characters to come out of this film genre. She also appeared in *How Much Land Does Man Need?* and several other dramas outside of the spaghetti-western world. She ended her acting career in 1983, joining an Indian mystic cult led by a man named Osho who has been active since the 1960s.

## Other Actors and Actresses

These were many spaghetti westerns made over the peak years for these films and, of course, there are many players who appeared in the casts. Many of them are international actors, so their names may not be that familiar to American audiences.

With these films, it's also important to keep in mind that there is a great deal of dubbing. Some of the actors you're hearing aren't actually the same actors that you're seeing but, in any international film genre, that's part of the fun and what makes the genre so distinctive.

## The Dollars Trilogy

The Dollars Trilogy is also referred to as the Man with No Name Trilogy. It consists of the three Sergio Leone movies where Clint Eastwood portrays the Man with No Name: *A Fistful of Dollars* (1964), *For a Few Dollars More* (1965), and *The Good, the Bad and the Ugly* (1966). The character unites this trilogy, not the story.

This trilogy of films doesn't need to be watched from earliest to latest. In fact, the films can stand on their own individually, be watched latest to earliest or in any other order and make perfect sense.

Watching the films from *A Fistful of Dollars* to *The Good, the Bad and the Ugly* may, in fact, introduce a bit of confusion.

In *For a Few Dollars More*, for instance, Lee Van Cleef plays Col. Douglas Mortimer, a bounty hunter who works with the Man with No Name to get El Indio. In *The Good, the Bad and the Ugly*, Van Cleef plays Angel Eyes, the main antagonist, who is in direct—and deadly—competition with the Man with No Name to find the $200,000 worth of gold that the three main characters are searching for.

Even in the case of the Man with No Name himself, there are some discrepancies that the audience will, no doubt, cotton to as they watch the films.

## The Man with Three Names

While he may be called the Man with No Name, the Man with No Name actually has three names in these films. In *A Fistful of Dollars*, he is referred to as "Joe," both by the undertaker in the film and in the ending credits. In *For a Few Dollars More*, the Man with No Name is referred to as Manco. In *The Good, the Bad and the Ugly*, the Man with no Name is called Blondie by Tuco. When the two are questioned by a Union captain as to their names, however, both fail to give any.

These films weren't intended to be a continuing saga, but the character is so similar between each of the films that most people regard them—and the films are marketed as—a trilogy. The connection comes from the look and attitude of the character.

## The Man with No Name's Traits

The Man with No Name tends to wear beat-up clothing, the trademark elements of which are his poncho, worn black jeans, a six-shooter in a brown leather holster on his right hip and a battered hat. He also wears a sheepskin vest in some scenes.

The Man with No Name is usually either chomping on or smoking a cigarillo. He oftentimes keeps his hands hidden beneath his poncho, only throwing the hem of it back over his right shoulder when he's about to draw. This hearkens back to the samurai roots of the character, as samurai often wore loose clothing that concealed their arms and their movement.

The Man with No Name is typically slow-moving and oftentimes downright laconic, until he's in danger, in which cases he moves with lightening swiftness and surprising agility.

The Man with No Name is an outlaw type and a deadly gunslinger, but he tends towards psychologically manipulating his adversaries when he can. Though certainly capable of handling himself—and then some—in a direct conflict, he's a very intelligent man who prefers to get the advantage by setting up his adversaries and nearly toying with them. As an example, the final duel with Ramon in *A Fistful of Dollars*, where the Man with No Name conceals an iron plate under his poncho and torments Ramon by refusing to die from repeated rifle shots shows how the Man with No Name likes to unsettle his opponents before moving in for the kill.

## An Icon

For many viewers, the Man with No Name was simply a breath of fresh air. He is a morally ambiguous character who looks like he just crossed a hostile desert rather than looking like he just crossed a movie studio lot, the latter being the case with many Hollywood protagonists. He is perpetually unimpressed and not intimidated, making one wonder what this man has been through and how it has tempered his nerves to a knife-like hardness. He says few words but, when he does speak, it always counts. The man wastes nothing. Bullets usually hit; words always have meaning; plans always have a profit for the Man with No Name at the end.

The character is also notable for his patience. He'll take days or weeks to execute a plan. When something offends his sense of right and wrong, he doesn't immediately react, guns blazing, to make it right. He might help a family being brutalized by the local thugs by sneaking them to the edge of town at night, handing them some money and telling them to get while the getting is good. He might stop for a moment, offer a dying soldier a cover to keep him warm and a few drags off of a cigarette for comfort in the soldier's last moments. He might blow up an entire bridge not only to make his plans easier, but to stop the senseless slaughter of soldiers who don't even understand why they're fighting over a useless bridge in the middle of nowhere.

The Man with No Name, despite his sometimes superhuman abilities, is very human, and that's what makes him so memorable. His actions aren't always comprehensible when seen through the lens of a guiding morality or even a guiding amorality. He does as he pleases, makes a handy profit doing it and, when he can, he helps out those who appeal to his sense of mercy. He's not a psychopath, as he does feel for people and seems to have a disdain for the bullies and thugs of the world. He's also not a softie, and he'll gun down an adversary in the fraction of a second it takes him to aim and fire.

You'll find many films summarized and analyzed in the following chapters, but there is something about Leone's Man with No Name Trilogy that is genuinely magical, for lack of a better term. While many spaghetti westerns are fine films, there are few that ascend to the sheer epic scale of Leone's Man with No Name Trilogy and there are few characters as memorable as The Man with No Name himself. Whatever you end up thinking of these three films, Leone's character and the way Eastwood portrayed him forever redefined the western hero. When watching the three films in this trilogy, be prepared to see one of the most incredible characters in any genre in some of the most engrossing western stories ever put on film.

http://movies.stackexchange.com/questions/353/does-it-matter-in-which-order-i-watch-the-man-with-no-name-trilogy

http://dollarstrilogy.wikia.com/wiki/Man_with_No_Name

## A Fistful of Dollars (1964)

### Director:

Sergio Leone

### Starring:

Clint Eastwood

Marianne Koch

There are so many great things that start with this film that it's nearly impossible to overstate its importance. This is one of the defining films of the spaghetti western genre. It also marks the debut of the Man with No Name, a character who is practically synonymous with spaghetti westerns. From its incredible direction to its sparse locations to its hard-edged, morally ambiguous lead, this film has it all, and more. This is a must-see for anyone who's interested in spaghetti westerns. It's worth seeing again for those who are already familiar with it.

### The Plot

This is not a feel-good western. It opens up with a sequence of a child getting shot at and another brutally kicked by a pair of Mexican bandits. The Man with No Name watches, seemingly indifferently, as he drinks from a well. He rides into town under a hangman's noose while a bell tolls mournfully in the distance, giving some indication of what the Man with No Name is. He's death and, immediately upon riding into town, he sees a dead man riding by on a horse. This is San Miguel and it's no place for any sort of decent person. Fortunately, the Man with No Name really isn't a decent person, so he'll fit right in.

It's not long after arriving that the Man with No Name demonstrates what he's made of. He's looking for money, just like everyone else in San Miguel, but he's not going to get started hunting down that money before having it out with some of the local thugs. The women of the town are all widows, according to the local barkeep, and a coffin maker busies himself outside the window of the tavern, apparently doing a tidy business for himself.

San Miguel is something of a stopping-off point for bandits. They do a good trade in guns and liquor but, of course, there's always a boss. There is more than one in this town, with the Rojo brothers and the Baxters—whose patriarch is the sheriff—each wanting to take over the own. The Man with No Name decides to pit the families against one another to his own gain. He offers his services to Don Miguel Rojo, but not for cheap.

The Man with No Name establishes himself as a capable killer in one of the most memorable sequences in the movie and one that really sets this character up for this film and for the others that follow. He casually asks the coffin maker to get three coffins ready, guns down the four Baxter men that harassed him when the Man with No Name came into town and then apologizes to the coffin maker for ordering too few coffins.

Most westerns would have set up the protagonist as an expert gunslinger and this one does, but this film goes farther. What we see is that, not only is the Man with No Name an impossibly efficient killer, he's also a master of psychological manipulation. He baits the bandits into the fight, knowing full well they don't have a chance against him. They're just pawns to help the Man with No Name execute his plan and, of course, a good chess player doesn't hesitate when it's time to sacrifice a pawn.

The Man with No Name doesn't take long to put his plan into action. The Rojos take a shipment of gold from a group of Mexican soldiers while dressed as American troops, taking the gold for themselves.

The Man with No Name sets up both families against each other. He tells each side that there are soldiers who survived the massacre and the Baxters and Rojos both want to get ahold of the survivors. The Rojos want to kill them to prevent any witnesses from testifying as to what happened and the Baxters want to get that testimony. The Man with No Name planned to steal the gold from the Rojos but his plans go wrong.

Marisol, a hostage held by the Rojos, becomes the focus of the plot. Her husband was gambling with Ramon Rojo and got accused of cheating. Ramon took his wife, but when the Rojo gang decides to gun down Marisol's husband, the Man with No Name steps in. No one wants to take on the Man with No Name. The Man with No Name helps the family, giving them money and telling them to get out of town with it.

This doesn't go over well with the Rojos, of course, and they capture the Man with No Name. He gets away, however, and the Rojos lash out against the Baxters, killing several of them. The Rojos now rule San Miguel, just as they'd wanted.

The final showdown in this movie pits the deadly Ramon Rojo against the Man with No Name. The Man with No Name wins based on both his wit and his speed, demonstrating again that it's his intelligence as much as his gun-slinging abilities that get him through life and, in fact, often make him the most efficient dealer of death.

## A Taste of Violence
The violence in *A Fistful of Dollars* will likely not seem that graphic to modern audiences, but it has to be considered within its era. This film was made outside the Hollywood studios, which enabled Leone to take risks where portraying violence was concerned. This film may not show the exploding blood, misery and graphic deaths that one would see in a modern film, but it shows the consequences of violence in ways that few westerns of the time—if any, really— dared to do.

This is most apparent not in the gun-fighting sequences themselves, but in the sequence where Marisol is being returned to her captors, the Rojos. Her child cries to see her, eliciting a feeling of compassion from the Man with No Name. Jesus and Julio, Marisol's son and husband, respectively, dare to meet her out on the street. It's not long before Julio is being threatened with death. The old barkeep steps in with a shotgun and, before one of the Rojos can draw, the Man with No Name steps forward, just slightly enough to let the thug know that he's not going to get away with gunning down the barkeep without catching a bullet himself.

This is where the ambiguity comes into play. The Man with No Name will not hesitate to gun you down and he's certainly not a good guy, but he does have a sense of going too far. He doesn't like what's going on with the Rojos and Marisol, and when the barkeep explains to him the entire story, the Man with No Name hits a limit. He ends up getting Marisol out of her captivity and sending her family on their way, showing that he isn't really the bad guy he might appear to be at times. He's self-motivated and deadly, but not a bad person. He even gives them money, the acquisition of which is the entire reason why he's risking his life playing two deadly families against one another.

When the Man with No Name gets violent, however, he's very good at it and it defines his character to a significant degree. He's faster than just about anyone he comes up against and never seems to break a sweat.

The massacre of the soldiers may not be that bloody—particularly since it involves a Gatling gun—and no horses die, but it's still way over the top for a movie of the time. Soldier after solider falls before the gun, making it almost seem like a World War I battle, with hapless infantry getting cut down like wheat before the most advanced weapons of the time. When one man tries to make a break for it on a horse, we get a taste of what Ramon Rojo can do with a rifle as he guns the man down with a single shot from a very long distance away.

The violence in this film, to no small extent, is really what it's about. This isn't a story of a white-hat gunslinger coming into town and making things right. This is a story about a mercenary type coming into town and figuring out a way to play two very powerful families against one another, to his own benefit.

There is a real sense of danger in this film. The Man with No Name cannot assume that his being the protagonist in the story means that he'll win every gunfight. He has to hide quite often and ends up nearly losing his life in the process of playing the families against one another. This is Leone's West. The bullets are real, the blood is real and the death is real, and that sense of danger is really what makes this western work. The scene where the Baxters flee their burning house, only to be gleefully slaughtered by the Rojos, is particularly brutal.

## Appreciating This Spaghetti Western
This film is a remake of *Yojimbo*, a Kurosawa samurai picture. Leone didn't have any rights to remake that film and, thus, *A Fistful of Dollars* was delayed to the box office because of a lawsuit. However, even though it might be a remake, it takes some interesting Japanese tropes, transplants them to the American West and ends up being an excellent film.

The Man with No Name is very much a ronin, a samurai who hasn't any employer. He's a lethal warrior, to the point of having skill that can only be described as legendary. Unlike most western heroes that came before him, however, he's not wearing impeccably clean clothes, riding a white horse and apparently availed of top-notch dental care. He looks like a creature of the frontier and his warrior nature means that his hands are thoroughly drenched in blood, something that he's quite comfortable with and knows how to profit from.

This character, of course, would become legendary in the following films in what are generally regarded as the Dollars Trilogy or the Man with No Name Trilogy; *A Fistful of Dollars, For a Few Dollars More*, and *The Good, the Bad and the Ugly*. The Man with No Name isn't quite fully formed here as a character, but all the basics are there. He's a bit more verbal and concerned than he is in some of the following movies. He wears a poncho, under which he keeps his hands and guns unless he's getting ready to shoot someone or lighting up a cigarillo.

This film may be a remake, but the plot works very well in the western setting. The drama between the two families is a perfect setup for a guy like the Man with No Name, who's always looking to make a profit, preferably at the expense of someone else. What makes this character so interesting, however, is that he's a predator that hunts other predators. Faced with the sympathetic family hardships of Marisol, Julio and Jesus, he opts to do what's right and get them out of town. This makes him a more redeemed character and one that the audience can identify with and genuinely like. If he were colder toward the family's plight, it would have been a lot harder to care about how things turned out, as it would have made him into the cleverest crook, but no one that anyone would really want to be.

Enjoying this film is not hard. It's incredible. The landscapes are breathtaking and huge, the town is dusty and mostly vacant and the people are hard and deadly. Words are few and, when they do come, they usually have plenty of meaning behind them, not wasting the viewer's time.

If you've not had the chance to watch Italian westerns, starting with *A Fistful of Dollars* and working your way through the Man with No Name Trilogy is a great way to get into the genre. These films are excellent all around and they are likely to be enjoyed by anyone, whether the person happens to enjoy westerns in general or not. For those who are really tired of the conventional westerns out there, this is a good film for demonstrating why so many people consider the Italian films in this genre to be the best and, among those films, this film is certainly one of the finest examples of filmmaking you'll find. Low-budget, sparse sets but great pacing and memorable characters make this film what it is.

## For a Few Dollars More (1965)
**Director:**

Sergio Leone

**Starring:**

Clint Eastwood

Lee Van Cleef

Eastwood and Van Cleef are bounty hunters in this second film in the Dollars Trilogy. While they'd both appear in *The Good, the Bad and the Ugly* as rivals, they're partners in this film and the two have quite a bit of on-screen chemistry that makes *For a Few Dollars More* even more enjoyable than it already is. Like most of Leone's westerns, this film is dark and violent and populates the West with some genuinely frightening characters. It also contains scenes that mirror scenes in *The Good, the Bad and the Ugly*, but on a less-epic scale.

## The Plot
The film opens up with a passage indicating that there's a very active trade in dead bodies at the time the film takes place. Bounty hunters range across the Southwest, hunting down wanted men and turning in their corpses to law enforcement to make a living. Among the worst of those wanted men is the villain El Indio, and Colonel Douglas Mortimer (Van Cleef) and Manco (Eastwood) want El Indio, preferably in a pine box.

Mortimer is introduced first and he's a tough, dangerous man. He's also surprisingly refined in some regards. He wears all black, having an almost clerical appearance. He's reserved and to-the-point and, though he's certainly intimidating and obviously a deadly man, he has an air of authority about him, which is fitting, given that he's a colonel.

We get a taste of Mortimer's skill when he guns down Guy Calloway, an outlaw he finds in Tucumcari. He starts looking for a man named Cavanagh, who has a higher bounty on his head, but also learns that the Man with No Name—called Manco in this film—already has designs on that outlaw and the $2,000 bounty on his head.

Manco manages to take out Cavanagh. At this point, it's apparent that both Mortimer and Manco are dangerous men and, of course, they're soon to meet one another.

Manco and Mortimer strike up a partnership, both agreeing to go after El Indio and the rest of the outlaws who run with the notorious bandit.

The two men need a plan more sophisticated than going in and gunning it out with the outlaws, so they hatch a scheme to get Manco into El Indio's gang. Manco gets one of the gang members out of jail, securing the trust of El Manco and getting a place in the gang.

Mortimer comes into play when the gang robs a bank in El Paso. They cannot open the safe, but Mortimer cracks the safe without blowing it up. They have to wait for the heat to die down from the bank robbery, so El Indio says that he'll stash the money and divide it up later. Of course, with that much money to go around, Mortimer and Manco decide that they're going to get it before the outlaws do. It doesn't go well and both end up getting caught. El Indio proves his worthlessness by faking the escape. Manco and Mortimer, send his gang after them to finish the two.

Mortimer is very clever, however, and he manages to get the money. The final showdown occurs in Agua Caliente—Hot Water, appropriately enough—when Mortimer and Manco gun down everyone that El Indio can throw at them. In the final showdown, El Indio and Mortimer face off alone, or so it seems, and El Indio manages to disarm Mortimer, apparently sealing his fate.

Manco shows up in the nick of time and, while holding El Indio at gunpoint, gives Mortimer his own pistol so that the duel is fair. Mortimer guns down El Indio.

It turns out that Mortimer had a personal motive in hunting down El Indio. El Indio had murdered his sister's husband, raped her and, while he was raping her, she killed herself. Mortimer doesn't want any of the bounty that he would have had coming and he and Manco part friends. In the end, Manco rides off with a wagon full of bodies, off to get a bounty of $27,000 dollars.

## Foreshadowing What's to Come

This film stands on its own as a fine western. In fact, it's a great western, but the connections between it and *The Good, the Bad and the Ugly* will be obvious to anyone who has seen that film and, in some ways, this film is a sort of a preview of some of the most iconic scenes in that film.

We get a bathtub ambush in the first sequences of the film, with Mortimer hunting down his first bounty of the movie. The difference is that the outlaw in this case is no Tuco. He shoots, but he misses Mortimer and flees out a window, eventually dying at the hands of the bounty hunter.

We also get a great preview of the three-way showdown at the end of *The Good, the Bad and the Ugly*. El Indio and Mortimer face off in a white stone circle under the blazing sun. Manco acts as a sort of referee in this shootout, rather than as a participant. As is the case with the Sad Hill shootout in the next film, there is plenty of staring, an elevating sense of tension and dread and the combatants are all fully capable of winning the shootout. This is a shootout that's going to be based on random chance more than skill; who draws first, who shoots straighter. Both of these men have done this plenty of times before, obviously, so there's no clear winner or loser at the outset, and Leone makes the most of that in how he builds the scene.

While Eastwood is really the star of the Dollars Trilogy, Van Cleef is in particularly good form in this film. The scene where he strikes a match using the suspenders of El Indio's hunchbacked gang member, Wild, is priceless. Mortimer knows he can outdraw the man. He knows he's deadlier and he's toying with the man, showing enough resolve to not flinch a bit when the man reaches for his gun a couple of times. This cold, confident attitude would be mirrored in the sadistic Angel Eyes character in *The Good, the Bad and the Ugly*. The difference is that Mortimer is a likeable character. Angel Eyes was a ruthless mercenary who didn't care who he killed. Mortimer is out to right a wrong and he's just plain cool. He's actually every bit as cool as the Man with No Name and it's rewarding to see Eastwood and Van Cleef play off of one another.

The Man with No Name is a bit more verbal than usual in this film. He's also, while still on the line between a good guy and a bad guy, more toward the good end of the spectrum. He's a tough customer, to be sure, but he's not so much an outlaw as he is in *The Good, the Bad and the Ugly*. In fact, he's actually working for the law in this film, though as a sort of independent contractor.

At the end of the film, Manco actually steps in and makes sure that things are fair. While the Man with No Name may have done the same in some cases, faced with a very similar situation at the end of *The Good, the Bad and the Ugly*, he knowingly put one participant in the final gun battle at a disadvantage and did so far in advance of the battle actually taking place. In both instances, however, the Man with No Name had a personal interest in doing so, making it less of a stretch for the character.

As far as Leone's style is concerned, it's on display here. Before a showdown, there are plenty of long stares. The music in this film, written by Morricone, is particularly eerie, consisting of only sharp whistles at times and, at other times, incorporating pipe organs and other odd instrumentations. As far as the music goes, it's the master at his best.

El Indio, played by Gian Maria Volonte, is a particularly haunting character. He carries a pocket watch that turns out to be integral to the plot of the film. It contains a picture of a woman who turns out to be Van Cleef's sister.

A flashback sequence shows El Indio stalking the young woman and her lover. He shoots down the young man and then forces himself on the woman, who grabs a gun and shoots herself through the heart, leaving a particularly gruesome wound. This scene is made absolutely nightmarish by the score in this film, which decays into dissonant chimes and bells during this sequence. It's a dark sequence in a movie that's already full of death and darkness. They way that it's carried out makes it even darker and, most certainly, far darker than anything you're likely to see in the average western.

This film really deals with one of the dirtiest professions in the Old West, the bounty hunter. In this film, and in many others, there are some discrepancies between the reality of being a bounty hunter and how it's portrayed in films.

## The Bounty Hunter with No Name

Bounty hunters make for great protagonists. One can assume they're handy with a gun and whatever other weapons they might need to get their work done, making their more outrageous feats of deadliness more believable. They're also likely to come into contact with the worst of the worst, which makes it easy to put them in perilous situations. Because they are, at least in the sense of employment, working for the law, they're characters that can be good guys, but that are also free to cross the line into being a bad guy when necessary. The way that they're portrayed in western films, however, including in *For a Few Dollars More*, has more to do with filmmaking and storytelling than actual history.

Bounty hunters oftentimes go after their targets with the understanding that they'll collect a handsome reward whether they bring the criminal back to jail or haul the criminal's dead body in on the back of a wagon, as the ending of *For a Few Dollars More* morbidly shows. In reality, most bounty hunters would have preferred to bring in a living, breathing criminal, as a dead body usually fetched only half the posted reward.

There are some legendary bounty hunters and, in *For a Few Dollars More*, two men who seemed more than capable of filling such shoes come into initial conflict, then cooperation. In reality, however, bounty hunters did not advertise themselves in the way that someone seeking a reputation as a gunslinger might. As one can imagine, bringing in members of violent gangs might just mark one for death among men more than willing to take an opportune shot, or hunt one down, just out of spite. In fact, according to Unusual Histories, bounty hunters didn't have their names recorded for their own safety.

In films like *For a Few Dollars More*, the bounty hunter operates with one goal: bring in the bad guy, no matter what doing so entails. In reality, bounty hunters did have to be more cautious than that and, if they could avoid shooting someone up, they stood to make more money. It was a profession that was likely to reward those who had good law enforcement skills rather than expert gunslinger skills, though both were likely useful at various times.

Nonetheless, as *For a Few Dollars More* demonstrates, the legendary bounty hunter character certainly makes for great entertainment!

## Appreciating This Spaghetti Western

*For a Few Dollars More* offers something a bit different than the other films in the Dollars Trilogy. In this film, the protagonists are thoroughly likeable and, in fact, seem to have a mutual respect for one another.

In *A Fistful of Dollars*, the Man with No Name is very much a ronin. He's out for himself, playing two families against one another and, essentially, working to bring them both down. This is entirely for profit motivation, though he does have his redeeming moments. In *The Good, the Bad and the Ugly*, we're treated to a story that reminds us that "good" is a relative term and Blondie is no good guy. He's a con man, a schemer and a killer. In *For a Few Dollars More*, both characters—Mortimer and the Man with No Name—are killers, to be sure, but the pure evil they're hunting down tends to give ample justification for what they're up to.

Mortimer is a sympathetic character. He lost his sister to an absolute monster and he means to set things right by gunning that man down. The Man with No Name is loyal, showing up to save Mortimer from suffering the same fate as his poor sister and being a bit confused as to why Mortimer would want to give up his cut of the profits from their enterprise at the end.

The Man with No Name is in fine form in this film. He's fast with his gun but just as fast with his mind. He's always a step ahead— most of the time, at least—and that makes him a survivor in addition to being a killer. Mortimer is pure class. He's a dark character, to be sure, and he doesn't mind intimidating his way to what he wants, but he's also on a mission that anyone could relate to. It might be about revenge, but it's revenge for all the right reasons.

This film has all the elements that a Leone fan will be looking for. It has the wide-open shots, the filthy saloon scenes and the characters always look like they live in the environments their stories take place in. The towns are sparse to the point of seeming nearly abandoned at points, but Leone manages to put together the action in a way where the lack of extras doesn't seem like it stems from low budgets, but from the fact that the towns in these films are places where no one in their right mind would want to be.

The villains are purely evil and they're not paper cutouts for the good guys to shoot at, avoiding another lacking element in many Hollywood westerns. In this film, the villains are alive because they happen to be better killers than anyone who's come after them, at least until Mortimer and the Man with No Name show up.

This film is a must-see and, even though one doesn't need to do so, it's rewarding to watch it second in line if you're taking in the entire Dollars Trilogy. You'll see elements of the Man with No Name character that don't line up with his character in other films, but you'll see plenty of elements that do. You'll also see some great foreshadowing of what Leone does in what many consider his finest film, *The Good, the Bad and the Ugly*, but it's much more than a dry run of that film. *For a Few Dollars More* is well worth watching whether you want to continue exploring Leone's vision of the West or not, though this film will probably persuade you to do just that.

http://unusualhistoricals.blogspot.com/2007/10/crime-punishment-bounty-hunters-in-old.html

## The Good, the Bad and the Ugly (1966)
**Director:**

Sergio Leone

**Starring:**

Clint Eastwood

Eli Wallach

Lee Van Cleef

*The Good, the Bad and the Ugly* is a Leone masterpiece set against the backdrop of the American Civil War. This film is notable for its characters, the incredible cinematography and direction and the soundtrack, which is likely the most distinctive and beloved soundtrack of this genre. This may be the third film in the Leone trilogy featuring the Man with No Name—known as Blondie here—but it is, according to many reviewers and fans, the best and one that is not to be missed.

### The Plot
While the way the film unfolds involves a lot of complexity, the plot is simple. Three men, none of them really meriting the appellation "the Good," are out to find $200,000 of gold buried in a cemetery.

One of the men, Blondie—ostensibly the Good—knows the grave that the gold is buried in. He may not have a name, but he has a huge body count to his credit and he's very capable, and willing, to add to it. He's intelligent, ruthless and deadly, but he's also the character in this film that shows the most capacity for compassion and fairness.

Tuco—the Ugly—is a Mexican bandit extraordinaire. Leone and Wallach play on the trope that characterized so many Mexican bandits in American movies, with Tuco oftentimes giving the impression that he's not too bright, but he does this to throw off his adversaries. A great example of this comes in the scene where a bounty hunter thinks he has the drop on Tuco when he finds the bandito taking a bath. Tuco is always ready, even if you think he's barely paying attention.

Angel Eyes, played by Lee Van Cleef, is the Bad in this film and he is most certainly a bad guy. He's about as cold as they come and he's not one to be toiled with. He's every bit as dangerous as Blondie and Tuco and, given that he also seems to be a bit more intelligent in many regards, he's even more so. Van Cleef gives an excellent performance in this film and truly embodies the shark-in-the-water role he's given.

This film is a long one, coming in at over 2 hours in total. Not a frame is wasted. The rambling storytelling style suits the subject matter.

Blondie and Tuco, at the outset of the film, have a scam going that nets them enough money to stay afloat. Tuco gets captured, Blondie collects the money for the bounty on Tuco and then frees Tuco, with both of them sharing the money. They have a sort of uneasy partnership going, until Blondie betrays Tuco.

Tuco gets his revenge, which ends up with the two of them discovering the existence of the gold from a man named Bill Carson. Angel Eyes already knows about the gold and Carson and is pursuing it himself.

Tuco and Blondie wind their way through their quest, running into Angel Eyes at one point and giving him the information he needs to get to the cemetery where the gold has been buried.

The end sequence is one of the most impressive that you'll see in any western. If you've ever thought that shootouts were too conventional in these films, that the characters approached them with all the dread of getting a hangnail removed, you'll think differently after you see the climax of this film.

A simple plot spawns an epic quest in this film. The characters wander through abandoned towns, towns that really should be abandoned based on the squalor alone, through deserts and military camps, and participate in Civil War battles.

What makes this film so good is that, despite it being easy to dismiss as another violent spaghetti western adventure, it's much more than that. There is real complexity in the characters and real reasons to be engaged with them.

## Nihilism in the Old West

The darkness in this film is perhaps best seen in one of its final sequences. Tuco, thinking he knows the name on the grave where the gold is buried, heads to the Sad Hill Cemetery to take it all for himself.

The cemetery is seemingly endless, taking up most of the wide-frame film. An enormous circle of graves, many of them obviously fresh, greet Tuco and he begins running through them, ecstatic. Appropriately, Morricone's "The Ecstasy of Gold" plays behind the scene, emphasizing the darkness and the irony.

This is a man whose entire life, at least as far as the audience knows, has been lived very close to death. He's either been a few steps ahead of it himself or been dealing it out, but these three characters are all practically incarnations of death. At Sad Hill Cemetery, Tuco has finally found the promise of everything he's wanted—wealth— amidst exactly what he most efficiently brings into this world.

The scene is dizzying. Tuco runs and runs, the music reaching glorious heights and the desert landscape constantly emphasizing the emptiness of the world that these characters live in. Not only do they put people in the grave, practically out of habit, but they have to dig up a grave to get what they want.

Tuco, always the impatient one, has assumed that he has more of a lead on his competition than is the case, and it's not long before Blondie shows up, followed shortly by Angel Eyes. What follows is beyond memorable. It's masterful. What makes it so incredible is that, if one were to lay it out on paper, it would sound like it would never work.

## Circle of Death

At the end of the film, it's apparent that one or two more graves are going to have to be dug in the Sad Hill Cemetery. The characters end up facing each other down, spread out across a broad cobblestone circle in the middle of the cemetery.

This is one of the most iconic shootout scenes of all, in any film, American or Italian. The tension is palpable. Tuco breathes hard, but he's not at all out of his league. He's fully capable of taking out both men. Angel Eyes looks cruel. His eyes are cold, calculating, lining up his shots. Blondie looks calm, but he's always calm and it's not apparent right away if he has an advantage or not.

The scene shows their guns. There are no hero weapons where. These guns are worn, used, grips chipped and worn. Even Angel Eye's hands show signs of wear, the tip missing from one of his fingers.

All of these men are capable of winning this three-way duel and all of them know it. There are no buffoons here. There are no examples of what video game players would call "trash mobs," disposable antagonists who are merely busy work until one reaches the final goal. These are all experienced, efficient and very professional killers.

In the end, Blondie has stacked the deck in his favor and in Tuco's, though Tuco doesn't quite see it that way. Blondie not only dispatches Angel Eyes, but he manages to drop him right in a grave, blasting the slain mercenary's revolver into the grave with him and ridding Tuco and Blondie of Angel Eyes once and for all. Almost comically, even in this instance, Blondie has gotten else to do the digging for him.

This goes on for nearly five minutes. The score, referencing Mexican trumpets, eerie bells and other odd instrumentation, raises the tension to almost unbearable levels. There is to be no happy ending here and, given that these are Italian westerns, not American westerns, there's no guarantee that the best guy is going to win and the worst guy is going to lose.

For this sequence alone, this film is worth watching, but there's far more to it than that. It takes true skill to raise tension levels this high, simply because the story and the direction have to make the viewer actually care about the characters by the time the story comes to a climax. Blondie is the most likeable character, but he's not a good guy, so he's more likeable on the antihero level than on the traditional hero level. Tuco is a very selfish, crass and not too bright guy, but he's cunning, clever, and admirable in his own way. Angel Eyes is the true badass. He's a killer through and through, merciless and calculating. He's not likeable, simply because he's so evil, but he's certainly someone that deserves respect.

## Appreciating This Spaghetti Western
*The Good, the Bad and the Ugly* is a bit unlike most trilogies. You can watch this film after watching *A Fistful of Dollars* and *For a Few Dollars More* or without watching those films at all and it's equally enjoyable. In fact, these films weren't actually designed to be a trilogy at all.

In this film, Eastwood is named Blondie. In the first and second films, he's known as Joe and Manco, respectively, so the character actually does have a name, but he's just as well known as Nameless or the Man with No Name.

This film actually takes place before the first two films chronologically, though it was released last. Some critics have pointed out that Eastwood's character, throughout this movie, gradually assembles himself into the character that would appear in the preceding movies. By the end of the film, Blondie has his entire distinctive outfit and rides off, presumably to wreak more mayhem, which is exactly the case, if one follows this line of thinking.

This film, however, is excellent in its own right. Many consider it Leone's best, better than *Once Upon a Time in the West*. Given that this film did have lower production values, the sets are sparser, there are fewer extras and there is less of a sense of things going on around the characters than one sees in *Once Upon a Time in the West*. This lends the film a somewhat eerier air to it, having the sense that many of these places have lived and died, just as the men who pass through them do, and that those places may have come and gone just as quickly.

*The Good, the Bad and the Ugly* is a long film. This is one that you'll likely want to stand up and get away from for awhile and come back to so that you can appreciate it in all its glory without being distracted by the runtime. It's well worth the investment of time and, as far as some viewers and critics are concerned, this is the finest western ever made. Even someone who doesn't particularly care for its dark tone or long story structure will likely have to concede that it is a great film, and one that deserves the praise that it gets.

## A Pistol for Ringo (1965)
**Director:**

Duccio Tessari

**Starring**

Giuliano Gemma (as Montgomery Wood)

Fernando Sancho

Hally Hammond

*A Pistol for Ringo* launched a successful sequel, relying on a charismatic leading man in Giulliano Gemma. The film doesn't have the darkness of many spaghetti westerns and, in fact, the title character is a friendly sort who just happens to be deadly with a revolver. The film has some fun with western tropes, such as when two tough guys meet one another on the street, stare at each other in silence for a moment and then shake hands, wishing one another Merry Christmas.

Ringo goes by the name Angel Face. It's not a ripoff of Angel Eyes, of course, this film predating *The Good, the Bad and the Ugly.*

The action gets into full swing when a group of banditos takes a ranching family hostage. The banditos are on the run and are being pursued, using a classic ploy to try to buy their freedom. The banditos will hold the ranching family hostage and demand that they be let go in exchange for the prisoners' lives.

Angel Face isn't exactly a good guy but, when things go wrong at the ranch, he's the best chance for the family to escape. The sheriff is at the end of his rope. He considers going into the ranch to save the family but, of course, he'd just get shot. None of the banditos knows Ringo and, of course, Ringo is a capable gunfighter, so they enlist his help. Ringo won't do it, until Ringo manages to figure out a way to make a profit out of the deal. He manages to get himself a percentage of the money that the banditos stole and the charges against him dropped.

Ringo gets in with the banditos, posing as one of them and even having a bit of fun partying with them. The sheriff works on getting cavalry to free the hostages while a representative of the interest that the banditos robbed worries about getting his money back.

Ringo's character gets revealed more and more as he interacts with the beautiful young daughter of the ranching family. He is most certainly a scoundrel of sorts and casually writes off his various murders as self-defense, but he's on the right side enough to constitute a good guy, for the most part.

Things go bad when the bandito leader starts executing hostages. Ringo pulls a double-cross on the bandito leader, Sancho, and manages to save the family, with the sheriff's forces coming down on the ranch.

### Lighter than the Norm

Ringo looks more like a Hollywood gunslinger than a spaghetti western gunslinger in this film. He's clean and neat, has perfectly straight, white teeth and is generally a happy-go-lucky sort, despite his inclination to get into deadly duels.

He is, however, morally ambiguous enough to fit the norm in these films. He's not a hard-hearted man like Angel Eyes or a sardonic, steely-eyed antihero like Blondie. He's more of a trickster-type villain, always getting a rise out of people around him and able to scheme and outthink his opponents to the point that he's always at the advantage. This guy seems to be in it for the action and adventure more than he is for the carnage and the gold, and that makes him a bit of a departure for many of these films.

Sancho, the bandito leader, does walk the fine line between frightening Mexican bandit and minstrel-show performer at times, as does his crew. The character doesn't go so far into stereotype territory that it becomes uncomfortable. He's a clever bandit, capable, ruthless and deadly. His men are sleazy and cruel, but no more so than any of the other villains in this film. Dolores, however, the female half of the bandito leadership, is a great character. She's obviously the brains behind the outfit and is as ruthless and cunning as any of the guys are. She's an interesting addition to the cast and manages to mix being very feminine and quite attractive with being as deadly as her profession would indicate.

The film has an interesting variation on plot for a western. Rather than a race after a buried treasure or a showdown at high noon, we get a hostage story, with the countdown being the time that Ringo has to get the hostages out of harm's way before the cavalry arrives and does what cavalry does best: kills everyone.

The Ringo character does a good job of going between appearing trustworthy and appearing that he has another plan going, but he ultimately does prove to be loyal enough to complete his mission. Wood is great in this role, playing a rather standard character but having enough fun with the role to keep it interesting.

### Appreciating This Spaghetti Western

There are some genuinely funny moments in this film. The banditos attempting to sing "Silent Night" is among the best, with them dutifully mumbling the words while the ranch owner's daughter plays away at the piano. Ringo is a fun character and, though he lacks the depth of some other spaghetti western heroes, he manages to be interesting and presents a lighter, less self-motivated character than one would expect to see in this genre.

The violence in this film is more dramatic than realistic. The interiors are brightly lit affairs and the costumes are immaculate. Even the characters that would normally be covered in dust, grease and sweat—such as the banditos, who have been riding long miles on the run—look like they just stepped out of the shower. The sheriff is squeaky clean, in particular, both ethically speaking and in terms of his overall look.

This film isn't the journey into darkness that many people will be looking for in a spaghetti western, but it's a good time. The gunfights are exciting enough, but there isn't the sense of danger that goes along with some of the more complex examples of these films. Sancho, for instance, wouldn't last a second against Tuco, the latter of whom presented the audience with a good idea of why banditos were people to be feared, while Sancho's ruthlessness seems more related to the plot of the film than the character simply being a self-motivated, murderous type.

This film does boast a score by Ennio Morricone, and the music is not surprisingly excellent. It's a lot less haunting than the scores he did for Leone's films, however, with the eerie drones and odd instrumentation being replaced by rather conventional orchestral themes, pizzicato strings that invoke the trotting of horses and other conventions.

That's not to say that this film doesn't have darkness in it. When one of the banditos decides to rape the ranch owner's daughter, the scenario is frightening and one feels for the character as she tries to flee into the night. Ringo, with characteristic slickness, confronts the would-be rapist and Sancho by pointing out that the rancher's daughter is part of what's keeping the ranch from being taken down by the cavalry. Ringo manages to duke it out with the rapist, giving the audience the satisfaction of seeing the man take a decent betting and, eventually, a knife to the chest. Unlike the violence in a lot of spaghetti westerns, in this film, it tends to be violence between people who have it coming and people who intend to collect on behalf of karma.

This isn't the darkest of the spaghetti westerns out there, but Wood manages to make it quite a bit of fun to watch and it definitely has its moments.

## The Return of Ringo (1965)
**Director:**

Duccio Tessari

**Starring:**

Montgomery Wood (Giuliano Gemma)

Some spaghetti westerns are epic, but there are few stories in this world as epic as those of Greek mythology. *The Return of Ringo* utilizes this to good effect, essentially being a revised version of Homer's *Odyssey*. Ringo, having finished his stint in the American Civil War, returns home to find that things are not as he left them and, in fact, that they're much worse than he could have imagined.

### The Plot
When Ringo makes it home at the beginning of this film, no one seems to recognize him. He's returned from the Civil War, still wearing his uniform, but the local bartender seems to think that he's someone else. Nearby, a couple of tough-looking hombres, apparently banditos, sit at a table listening to the conversation and playing with a knife.

The bartender reveals that Ringo is dead, partially for the benefit of the banditos at the table, who seem to be very interested in learning more. Ringo plays along, mentioning his wife as if he didn't know her. He realizes what's going on and turns around, gunning down both of the banditos with frightening efficiency.

The bartender lets Ringo know what's up. Banditos have taken over the town and his wife has become engaged to the leader of the gang. No one dared stand up to the banditos. Of course, Ringo is back in town now, so that's likely to change soon.

Ringo, however, ends up with a bad case of the thousand-yard stare when he finds out about his wife. He comes up with a plan, however. He disguises himself as a peasant, allowing himself to get access to the banditos, who claim that the town is now Mexican territory.

Before any unpleasant notions of blackface come to mind, it's not like that. Ringo is not trying to imitate a Mexican for racist comedy. Ringo needs to get access to the people who have, apparently, stolen everything he cared about and to do that he has to ditch the blond hair and pale complexion that would make him an instant outsider.

In the town, the only things on the street are wind, blowing debris and people who are soon to join the dead themselves. A man is gunned down right in front of Ringo and no one even notices.

*The Return of Ringo* follows in the tradition of other Italian westerns in that the Mexican bandito characters are intimidating from the start. These aren't comical buffoons who wandered up from the south to displace the more capable American gunslingers. These guys are dangerous to the core; they're hard, ruthless and always looking for a reason to kill someone. They insult Ringo right away and Gemma pulls the scene off masterfully. This character cannot intimidate his way out of this situation the way that the Man with No Name or Angel Eyes may have. He has to keep everything close to the chest and, for a man as deadly as Ringo, that has to be tough.

Ringo's old town has become utterly lawless. Americans are considered inferior in the town. What's going on isn't just some banditos rolling into town and causing havoc. These are organized, nationalistic and violent thugs who intend not only to push their way around the town, but to rule it utterly, and they've apparently succeeded.

Hallie is Ringo's wife and the object of desire for Fuentes, the leader of the Mexican thugs. Fuentes wants to marry her but, of course, she's married already. Ringo gets a job with the local florist, a busy profession given the number of funerals in this town, and one that provides some foreshadowing.

Morning Glory, the florist, relates to Ringo how the young men of the town were away fighting in the Civil War when the banditos showed up. There was no one there to fight the banditos and, when someone did come back and try to fight, they inevitably ended up being killed by the bandits.

Ringo's barely contained rage is part of what drives this film. When Esteban, one of the leaders of the gang, tries to deal out some justice by way of roughing up Ringo for insulting a Tarot-reading femme fatale, Rosita, Ringo takes a beating, but nearly manages to take out the cadre of banditos beating him down as well. Rosita picks up on the fact that Ringo is curiously unafraid of the banditos and that he's packing a gun, though he refused to use it.

Ringo awakens after spending the night in a trough to see his own funeral procession going down the street. He's buried as a war hero, opening up the way for Fuentes to marry his wife. This, to put it lightly, is the straw that breaks the camel's back. He sees his wife and daughter, the latter of which has his bright blonde hair, as well as the leaders of the gang who have decimated his town and his life in general, and there's real hate in his eyes in this scene.

Fuentes, however, makes a serious error before tossing the first handful of dirt on Ringo's grave. He says that they won't see Ringo again, but they certainly will. A man in a Union uniform is seen taking a bribe for having put on the funeral.

Ringo starts to work out a plan and to prepare for battle. The first sequence established that he's more than capable of killing a man and, given his rage, it's obvious that far more than one man is going to die before Ringo's done.

The sheriff recognizes Ringo after he beats the stuffing out of a group of thugs, including the notorious Esteban, without breaking a sweat. Morning Glory gets in on the action, too, making the accusation that Esteban was breaking the law. Ringo is not only taking revenge, he's rallying the whole town to the cause.

Ringo executes a plan, styling offing some of the banditos, getting others thrown in jail and sneaking dynamite into the ranch where the wedding is to be held. Fuentes comes into town to see filled coffins in the church, courtesy of Ringo.

Fuentes is genuinely frightened when Ringo appears in full Union regalia, packing a rifle and a pistol at the church door. He realizes the coffins contain his own men and, running out to confront the apparent ghost, he watches as Ringo guns down his thugs with the help of some of the townspeople and a Native American warrior and mystic well known to the townsfolk.

Ringo continues to inspire the townsfolk after they drive the banditos out of town. Hallie is back with Ringo, but there's still a fight coming and they know it. Rosita, though she freed Esteban and got the sheriff killed, is quickly forgiven by Ringo and becomes one of them. Ringo still has to rescue his daughter, and he's not about to fail.

A gunfight as epic as this genre is notable for ensues, with the townsfolk helping Ringo to drive the bad guys out. Ringo makes his way around the ranch stealthily, taking out anyone unlucky enough not to see him coming, and gets his daughter back. Ringo's daughter, rather than being the usual screaming motivation for the protagonist, is rather amusing, apparently sharing her father's steel nerves and not even flinching when he guns down armed men right in front of her. She even demonstrates that she knows how to eject spent rounds from a revolver while the two hide in the attic.

A long fistfight with Fuentes follows, where the two are shown to be almost equally matched. Almost. Ringo guns Fuentes down, solving the town's problems in the most western way possible, with Fuentes eventually making it out the door to be taken down in a hail of gunfire from the townsfolk.

## What Makes This Film Work

This film, by many measures, is much more engaging than *A Pistol for Ringo*. It's darker, the tone is more morbid and the violence is more realistic, by far. While *A Pistol for Ringo* does have its moments, the hero always seems to be having fun with the situation at some level and getting a kick out of staying a step ahead of the law and the antagonists. In this film, he's much different.

Ringo in this film is sometimes explosive, indicating the rage he's barely keeping inside. Rosita is a good foil for this, wanting to ask the cards what the truth of this man is but being shut out at every opportunity. She's also something of a foil for the townspeople. They gave up and stopped fighting the bandito gang, much to their detriment but, as Ringo says, everyone makes mistakes.

This film has some very tense moments. It plays on the fact that the audience knows that Ringo could probably cut his way right through his adversaries if he were able to divide them up into smaller groups, but the tension comes from the fact that he's unable to do that. He's going to need help and the townspeople have plenty of courage to lend. They just needed someone to lead and inspire them, which Ringo does to great effect.

The banditos in this film are very effective. They're experienced killers like Ringo, and it's not because they're easy kills that the townspeople eventually win the day. The banditos are arrogant and sadistic and that is ultimately their downfall. Confronted with people who are neither intimidated nor particularly impressed, they're unable to overcome the inspiration to fight that takes over the townsfolk and are eventually driven out or killed, with most of them suffering the latter fate.

The film ends abruptly, with a jarring shot of a happy family walking away together across a killing field littered with corpses. The happy scene is made a bit less jarring, however, by the fact that the good guys do win in this one, and the bad guys get driven right into the ground.

## The Town
The town in this film is something of a character in and of itself. There isn't any activity on the streets, the stores are largely abandoned and the saloon is generally just full of banditos and no

one else. At all times, a wind blows through the town, kicking up dust and tumbleweed, straw and grit.

The town is classic for an Italian western, whose low budgets oftentimes restricted the amount of extras that were on the set creating background activity. In this movie, it fits very well. The town is dead, as are most of the people in it. It's a hopeless, forlorn place, but Morning Glory's garden is one bright spot showing that the town could bloom again, if it had the right person to tend to it.

## Appreciating This Spaghetti Western
This film deals with themes of death and vengeance, familiar ones for anyone who likes spaghetti westerns. It doesn't hurt one bit that it draws on such highly regarded source material, of course, and that makes it even more engaging.

In the first Ringo film, the protagonist seemed like someone who was nearly impossible to beat down. He faced death with a smile, was always working an angle to benefit himself and was clever enough that one could be certain he could outwit or outshoot just about anyone he came across. That's not the case in this film.

Ringo, in this film, is a tired solider who is returning home, thinking that the war is over and finding out that there's one last battle he has to fight. After surviving one of the most horrific wars in U.S. history, he's got to face down a bunch of banditos who have decided to make his town into their personal lair.

The banditos put on airs, with their leader fancying himself a Don, a Spanish nobleman who would have typically controlled a lot of land and political power. He's really just a thug, however, and the most ruthless and powerful thug among his lot. They may want to make the town into Mexico, but they're not Mexican soldiers. They're just slick gangsters looking to take what they can and, hopefully, to make as many people as they can miserable in the process.

This film is really quite good, and for audiences that like their westerns a bit darker and more complex, it will likely outdo the original *A Pistol for Ringo*. Gemma is very effective as a western hero and he's a bit nobler—considerably nobler, in fact—than the protagonists in Leone's films.

If you find the first Ringo film to be too light for your tastes, try this one. The film is rewarding in terms of the plot, Gemma is a lot of fun to watch and Rosita is an excellent character who makes a rather mysterious exit at the end of the film. Overall, this should make any viewer glad they took the time to watch it and it will definitely scratch the itch when one needs to take in a spaghetti western.

## A Bullet for the General (1966)
## Director:

Damiano Damiani

**Starring**

Gian Maria Volonte

Klaus Kinski

*A Bullet for the General* is a Zapata western, set during the Mexican Revolution. The story follows Bill Tate and Chuncho, an American gangster/assassin and a Mexican revolutionary as they make their way to General Elias to sell him arms to keep the revolution going.

**The Plot**

Bill Tate has been riding trains carrying firearms, waiting for notorious bandito Chuncho to raid one of them. When Chuncho finally comes, he poses as a man on the run, with a price on his head, from the United States.

Chuncho starts calling Tate "Nino," a reference to his boyish looks. Nino accompanies Chuncho's gang as they rampage across Mexico, taking on the military whenever the opportunity presents itself and bringing their load of looted guns, including a gold machine gun of which Chuncho is particularly proud, to the general.

The story is a violent one, with the bandito gang capturing and executing soldiers without hesitation and, eventually, taking over the lands of a local Don, whom they summarily execute in a nearby village. Nino manages to stop the men from raping the Don's wife, leading Chuncho to shoot one of his own banditos.

Chuncho tries to teach a group of peons to shoot, but it becomes apparent right away that these people are farmers, not fighters, and he gives up, heading back to join his comrades, including Nino, who have left the village with the guns, heading to meet the general.

The banditos make to the general, at which point Chuncho makes his sale, netting Chuncho 5,000 pesos. The general, however, is outraged that the guns Chuncho sold him were taken out of the village that Chuncho's banditos had liberated, leaving the village open to attack. The general reveals that soldiers raided the village after Chuncho left, and the government forces slaughtered most of the villagers. The general sentences Chuncho to death for betraying his countrymen for money, with El Santo, Chuncho's fanatically religious brother, agreeing to carry out the execution.

In the meantime, Nino sets himself up on a high ridge with a clear shot at the general. He kills the general and kills El Santo as he rides away, stopping Chuncho from being executed.

Before Chuncho and Nino had parted ways, Nino had told Chuncho that they should meet at a particular hotel in Juarez. Nino collects $100,000 in gold pesos from the government for his service. Chuncho waits for him, intending to assassinate Nino, but is persuaded to take his half of the gold.

Nino has clearly taken to Chuncho and wants to go back to the United States together, now that Chuncho is a rich man, even by U.S. standards. As they get ready to board the train, Nino explains how everything he told Chuncho was a lie and was only designed to get Chuncho to take Nino into the bandito gang, giving Nino access to the general.

Chuncho's revolutionary spirit comes out and he shoots Nino as the train is leaving. He leaves his share of the gold on the train station platform, telling a peon who picks it up to go buy dynamite, and runs off into the rail yard, either to his freedom or to his death. The movie ends with Chuncho screaming wildly, smiling and every bit the bandito he always was.

## The Romantic Revolution

*A Bullet for the General* is generally regarded as one of the better Zapata westerns out there and it does certainly play on some of the tropes in other films of this genre.

El Chuncho and his gang of banditos treat the revolution like a non-stop party. These are clearly people who are used to killing and, by any measure, are very good at it. They take on trained soldiers, using lightning-fast raids and guerilla warfare tactics to disrupt, divide and take down the solider units, hooting and hollering all the while.

The banditos roll through the Mexican desert like a group of nomadic warriors. They take shelter in whatever towns they liberate, and anywhere else that suits them. They go between violent raids and drinking binges, with the banditos having varying degrees of loyalty to, and various reasons for being loyal to, the revolution.

El Santos, played by Kinsky, is Chuncho's brother. He's a religious fanatic who despises the Mexican government and who is very much a revolutionary, right down to the core of his being. El Chuncho, by contrast, is a born fighter. He revels in conflict, is fast with his guns and easy to let go of someone when they die. When he shoots down his own man to protect Nino, his reply is a flat acknowledgement that the man, even though he was Chuncho's friend, is dead. Chuncho is quick to go on with his life.

Nino is driven to make it to the general. He's carrying a golden bullet—far more symbolic than realistic, as gold is not known for being good bullet-making material—which he intends to assassinate the general with.

El Chuncho is something of a legend in the making among the peons that he liberates. While he's no intellectual heavyweight, he does see the peons as people just like him, something that he says literally at one point. He might not be a scholar of Marx and Engels, but he gets the spirit of what they were saying and, despite the fact that he's an egotistical sort, he doesn't much care for people being oppressed.

This film is very political and does romanticize the Mexican revolutionary to no small extent. When the banditos go on raids, triumphant Mexican-inspired music plays, heralding the coming of justice. The violence, however, is rather brutal, making the scenes somewhat jarring. The film makes no bones about celebrating the deaths of solider after solider, sometimes in battle and sometimes in on-the-spot executions orchestrated by Chuncho and his banditos.

Adelita, a Mexican revolutionary woman who fights with Chuncho's gang, is somewhere in between the cynicism of Nino and the fiery spirit of El Santo. She and Nino are attracted to one another, but Nino doesn't want any complications. She's a brave fighter, however, running out in the middle of battles at times to deliver ammunition to her comrades, and a good soldier in her own right.

Chuncho is an experienced killer and an effective leader, but he's naïve. In some ways, this could be seen as symbolizing the revolution itself. When he tries to make soldiers out of peons, he finds out soon enough that they're more enamored with him than the revolution and that they're just not capable of fighting for themselves. He overlooks some rather big red flags about Nino, including the golden bullet that he finds in Nino's belongings, almost desperate to like the man. At some level, it seems like having an American along to watch the exploits of the Mexican banditos feeds into Chuncho's ego. When Chuncho meets the general, he finds a man much like any other land-owning Don of the time. The general is immaculate, has people who work for him and has a trunk full of money at the top of the high tower where he situates himself, well above the revolutionary rabble on the ground.

Chuncho accepts his death sentence for leaving the village he liberated unarmed without much emotion. He may be enamored with the revolution, but he's equally enamored with the general and doesn't question the unfairness of the sentence. After all, what would have been the point of arming a bunch of peons who couldn't shoot, anyway?

In this regard and some others, *A Bullet for the General* does have something of a cynical core to it. It might be fascinated with the Mexican Revolution and ready to make heroes out of the bandito gangs that contributed some of the muscle to it, but this revolution, like many others, really comes down to leaders and followers and the leaders of any revolution are oftentimes as detached from the reality of the people they claim to be fighting for as is the government the revolutionaries are fighting against.

One of the most tragic things about Chuncho is that he's so proud of his gold machine gun, but the general's people aren't phased by it at all. It's just another gun. All of the work, bloodshed and loss that went into getting that gun to the general culminate in the general's man indifferently nothing the machine gun in his ledger and then resuming counting the regular Mausers that Chuncho brought in for the general's cache.

## You Become What You Fight

There is a moment in this film, while the banditos are raiding a military barracks, when El Santo shows some rather raging hypocrisy. Of all the characters, his is the most motivated by the idea of exercising justice against the government and its troops. Those troops, and the government they work for, are brutal, in fact, and there is every indication that, despite the hardship the viewer sees on-screen being brutal, it's even worse off-screen.

When raiding the barracks, El Santo discovers a group of peasants being held in a below-ground cage where they're begging for water. He frees the men and then intervenes when Chuncho's men are about to execute a group of officers. Saying he has a "better way," El Santo throws the officers into the hole and lets them know that they're going to die very slowly.

While there may be some sense of turnabout being fair play in this, it's also just as brutal that anything the military does. El Santo, in this scene and others, shows himself as a man who sees divine fury and permission in his acts, no matter how brutal or cruel they may be and no matter how much suffering they may cause.

In many regards, this movie is about vengeance more than it is about justice. It's a thrilling ride, to be sure, but it's also very much coming at the viewer from a political angle. That angle holds that the oppressed, having suffered injustice at the hands of a brutal regime, are justified in being that brutal themselves, with summary executions and taking pleasure in slaughtering other men being celebrated throughout much of the film's runtime.

## Enjoying This Spaghetti Western

This is a politically charged film, but one that has a lot of the best qualities of the spaghetti westerns. It has the gritty look and feel, the rather ambiguous protagonists and plenty of violent action. In fact, this film has a lot of action in it, which should keep those who watch this genre for thrills very happy.

El Chuncho is a great character and, in some ways, he carries this film more than does Nino. Nino has a plan and he's a shady character, for sure, and that does make him interesting. What's almost more interesting, however, is watching how Chuncho becomes some fascinated with this man, whom he wants to be friends with but who ultimately plots against him. Chuncho is truly naïve in many regards. He takes care of Nino when Nino gets sick, much as one might expect someone to take care of a sibling and that seems to be how he views Nino.

Nino can be seen as a representation of American intervention in Latin America or as a character that represents capitalism. In either regard, he's cold, lies habitually and, at the root of it, he's only involved in any of this for the gold. He gladly guns down Mexican soldiers with Chuncho's prized gold machine gun, but he's actually working for the same side. The man puts Blondie and Tuco to shame where having no sense of loyalty is concerned and, in many regards, he's just downright sleazy. He's an assassin, a businessman of sorts and a slick customer who knows how to manipulate. He's also something of a war tourist, unattached to the people around him and only treating them like equals—or pretending to think of them as equals—when there's something in it for him.

In the end, despite his allusions to wanting to be Chuncho's friend, it's easy to believe that Nino just wants someone as a friend in the way that someone would want something from a tourist shop in a border town. Chuncho gets some clothes and a shave and haircut at

Nino's suggestion, with Nino trying to make a real-to-the-core revolutionary into a sort of pet revolutionary who's cleaned up and safe for the U.S.

It doesn't work, however, and that may be one of the strongest messages in this film. The Mexican Revolution, complex and bloody as it was, was really fought by peons and peasants against a corrupt government and system of Dons that controlled the land and that kept the people poor, uneducated and landless. It was a feudal type system that had little tolerance or accommodation for human rights and dignity. While Chuncho may not be the most dignified character, he does see himself as one of the oppressed and is more than willing to do what he does best—kill and loot—on their behalf. He even helps a village elect a mayor by finding the one man among the peons who can read and write, though it ends badly for the villain.

Nino may have thought he was like Chuncho and the two could be friends, but Chuncho knew better. Chuncho, once he catches on, knows who his enemy is and the slick, murderous and lying gangster from the U.S. fits the bill, earning Nino several shots in the chest and Chuncho his dignity back. Chuncho didn't care a whit about the gold, except that the people could buy a lot of dynamite with that money.

# Django (1966)
## Director:

Sergio Corbucci

## Starring:

Franco Nero

*Django* launched a successful character that would appear in several other films. In the opening credits of this film, we're immediately made aware that this is an Italian western, with a dirty, disheveled Django dragging a coffin down a lonely road, setting him up as a rather morbid protagonist from the start. The film's opening sequence features a song that was reused by Tarantino in *Django Unchained*, an indication that *Django* has some fans in very high places in the movie world.

## The Plot

*Django* opens up with a woman being brutally beaten by a group of bandits. He guns them down, saving the woman. The bandits work for the big bad in this film, Major Jackson, and Django has a grudge to settle with the major. The major murdered Django's wife and he wants to settle the score.

The major is a brutal character who leads an impressively large group of bandits. He's a refined guy, but a sadistic one who sells protection and amuses himself shooting down people as they try to run away. The man is stone cold to the core.

The major's men wear red sashes as a gang identifier. One of them starts beating a prostitute in a saloon, angering Django, who calmly tells the man to leave the girl alone. This catches the attention of the major, who identifies him as the "Yankee" who killed five of the major's men.

The Civil War might be over, but the major has worked up another war with a group of Mexican banditos. He picks a fight with Django in the saloon, finding out in a flurry of gunfire that Django is not to be trifled with and that he's not dragging a coffin around for his own use.

Django might be 100 percent pure gunslinger, but he has a sense of honor. He allows the major to walk away from the gun battle where he slaughters his goons, telling the major that he better round up all of his men for the major's own protection.

Django is a loner, but he gets warned that he can't do this by himself by Nathaniel, a friendly older guy who doesn't have any love for the major, but he's smart enough not to try to make any trouble. Django could leave at this point, but Django does need to finish the job. It's not long before the major rides back into town with some new thugs for Django. They wear red hoods this time, looking a little Klannish, and providing a nice contrast to the Union blues that Django still wears. They even set a cross on fire, giving some indication that there are plenty of reasons not to like these guys at all.

At this point in the film, it's hard to figure how Django is going to take out 20-plus men with a six-shooter. Of course, this is an Italian western and one doesn't drag a coffin around for symbolic purposes alone. It happens to contain a machine gun, which Django goes full-Rambo with, hoisting it up to his waist and slaughtering enough men to fill the street with bodies.

The major gets dumped off his horse into the muck. Django isn't just looking to kill to get revenge; he wants to drag this out and make it as humiliating as possible.

There is one other group of Big Bads in this film, the Mexican banditos, and it's not long before they come into town to fill the power vacuum that Django created with his machine gun. There are plenty of them to go around and they're a force to be reckoned with. They're also the mortal enemies of the major and they brutally torture and kill one of the major's men who they catch hanging around town. The scene will be familiar to anyone who's seen *Reservoir Dogs*, but it's even more brutal. These banditos don't just cut off your ear, they stick it in your mouth and shoot you in the back when they're done.

Unfortunately, these are the same men who were brutally beating Maria at the beginning of the film, and they want her back.

Django quickly engages in a bit of Man With No Name-esque playing of both sides. Django offers to help the general, the leader of the banditos, who's already a friend of his. He shows the general the machine gun he used to kill the major's men. He shoots up the saloon to show off the firepower to the general and offers to help him get nine more guns of the same type.

Django helps the banditos to get the gold from a nearby fort where Nathaniel brings prostitutes on a regular basis. The general, however, isn't in any rush to share the gold, so Maria and Django take it for themselves. They lose the gold and get caught by the general's men, who break Django's hand.

The banditos' plan doesn't quite work out, and they end up falling to Mexican army troops. The major catches up with Django, but Django outguns them all in one of the more interesting gunfights in Italian westerns, all against the backdrop of a cemetery.

## This Man Has a Name

There are some similarities between the story in *Django* and other Italian westerns. There are also some notable similarities between the title character, though he also stands on his own as one of the really great characters in Italian westerns.

Django is a bit more approachable than the protagonists in Leone's westerns, for the most part. In fact, he can be downright friendly to people who've done him no wrong and who don't seem about to. He keeps his word, whether he's promised himself that he's going to kill you or promised someone that he'd risk his life in a daring raid to get a pile of gold. He expects others to do the same.

While the Man with No Name might be entirely self-motivated with moments of loyalty or compassion making him more human, Django is really out to right wrongs. He's not in it for the money. In fact, he earns the enmity of the banditos by gunning so many of them down in the opening fight and got nothing for his trouble except doing the right thing and helping out someone in need.

Some of the scenes where Django does throw down are surprising for a western. In a genre where most of the actors fistfight like actors rather than real fighters, Django proves himself to be quite a creative and capable fighter. The character brawls with one of the general's men and it's not just sloppy western haymakers. The fight is genuinely brutal, eventually involving a pickaxe, and the combatants do a good job of tearing apart the bar as they try to beat one another down.

Django can't see Maria as a prostitute. He's not that cold. When he's offered the woman as a reward for saving the general—for the second time—he opts for another woman instead, but doesn't want to have sex with her. He gets ready to make the grab for the gold, something that is facilitated by the fact that the banditos are stinking drunk and distracting themselves with the company of prostitutes.

Ringo also keeps his soldier vibe throughout the film. It's easy to believe that he's as deadly as he's portrayed in the film, given that he survived one of the most brutal conflicts in history and seems to be utterly fearless. He's nearly workmanlike in the way he pulls off his tasks, whether they involve gunning down a gang of thugs or stealing a pile of gold.

There is a bit of creative license in this film, aside from the fact that Django hip-fires a huge machine gun with startling accuracy and no jams, despite it apparently being Civil War technology. The coffin full of gold that Django drags away would have likely been unmovable for him. He not only drags it off, he lifts it up single-handedly. Of course, the gold would have weighed a fantastic amount and it would be nearly impossible for one man to move it, much less lift it. Nonetheless, this is easy enough to overlook given the quality of the film.

In the end, it's hard not to enjoy Django, whether one is talking about the movie or the man. Nero is excellent as a western hero and this character is a fun one to watch. He has the tough-guy elements that make Italian western protagonists popular but it's tempered with sympathetic elements that make him a very relatable guy.

## Appreciating This Spaghetti Western

Django is an intensely likeable character. There really aren't any moments in this film where you have to forgive him for who he is, because he's essentially a good guy. He's a killer, to be sure, and he's very good at it. He kills for the right reasons, however, and the people he manipulates are savage thugs or slick gangsters of one sort or another, so it's not like he's killing people who have nothing to do with what's going on. Killer, yes, murderer, no, to put it in the plainest terms.

When he returns to Nathaniel's saloon with a badly wounded Maria, he's genuinely worried about her. He has the capacity to care for people, making him less distant than some of the protagonists in these films. In fact, in the end, he puts off taking off with Maria because he has to kill Jackson, not out of simple revenge, but because there can be no peace for Django or anyone he cares about unless the major is dead.

The filming style here is also excellent. We're treated to the same sparse, ramshackle sets that anyone who loves this genre will be well accustomed to. The streets are thick with muck, everyone seems to be dirtied by it and the saloon doesn't seem like the kind of place where you'd want to have a drink without wiping the grease off the glasses first.

Django's martial abilities may frequently range to the realm of superhuman, but that's part of the fun with this character. He's so deadly that going up against him is the definition of a fool's errand and the man holds a grudge and can't seem to let it go until it's satisfied. That can be seen as a character flaw or it can be seen as an indication of old-school honor.

The villains in this film are also effective. We essentially get two types for the protagonist to deal with. The general's banditos are Mexican revolutionaries and the types that use lightning-fast raids, overwhelming violence and intimidation to get what they want. The major's men are more organized and disciplined, but just as cutthroat and brutal. This provides an easy way for Django to set up the groups against one another, though it's not as much a part of the plot as it is in other Italian westerns.

The final shootout scene in this film is really something to remember. It's unique and the setup to it, disabling the hero by having his hands broken, gives it a lot more tension than many other shootouts. We're well aware of the fact that Django is a lethal gunslinger, but take away his hands and what does he have? His brain. He improvises to great—and rather morbid—effect.

There is a reason that Tarantino chose this film's theme to open up his own love letter to spaghetti westerns, as well as the name of the protagonist himself. In Tarantino's films, there are usually parts where someone is given a lecture—the audience, of course—about movies they should appreciate. It might be Tarantino going on about the brilliance of Jerry Lewis, how an actress looks like Lana Turner or something else, but it's usually in there. *Django Unchained* plays particular homage to *Django*, and for good reason. This is a film about a hero who isn't waiting for justice to catch up with the people who've wronged him, who's deadly with a firearm and who is one step ahead of the people who want him dead, making it a classic of the genre, and a film that spawned a host of films that were supposed, but unofficial, sequels. It's violent, it's dirty and it's intense, and that's what makes *Django* work. Franco Nero had a cameo in *Django Unchained*, leaving little doubt as to Tarantino's feelings on this particular film.

# Navajo Joe (1966)
**Director:**

Sergio Corbucci

**Starring:**

Burt Reynolds

Nicoletta Machiavelli

*Navajo Joe* will make you hate the antagonists in this film within a few minutes of the opening scene. Like many Italian westerns, this production gives the audience an unconventional hero in the form of the title character, played by Burt Reynolds, who does claim some Native American heritage himself. The film is a revenge tale, with Joe riding out to seek vengeance on a particularly brutal—inhuman, actually—group of bandits.

## The Plot
It's not hard to find atrocities in the Old West and this film opens up with an example of what Native Americans faced as the U.S. started moving into their territory. A group of apparently friendly Native Americans is going about their daily routine when one of the women encounters Duncan, the leader of a gang of thugs. He watches her passively for a moment while she smiles and offers no sort of hostility, then guns her down and scalps her. The rest of Duncan's men slaughter the entire village, which doesn't even have time to react to the attack.

It turns out that this is the worst idea that Duncan has probably ever had and things go south for him quickly. He spots a lone native, mounted on a horse, standing atop a high mesa and sends two of his men after the man. It doesn't go well for the outlaws. The rider utterly overwhelms them, taking out one of the riders in a fast hand-to-hand exchange and gunning down the other before he can even raise resistance, knocking the man off his horse with a rifle butt.

It turns out that Duncan is half-Indian himself and he resents it. His men come back on one horse, one of them sporting a knife wound and the other shot to death.

Duncan is a complete psychopath. When he sees wanted posters, he wants to punish the townsfolk in the town where they're posted for having hung them up in the first place. His men tear up the town, brutalizing everyone they meet and darkening the atmosphere at what seemed like a pretty fun saloon before they all showed up.

The outlaws have the disposition of a group of drunken Vikings. They take what they can, burn what they can't and kill anyone unfortunate enough to get in their way. Even the sheriff won't take the scalps that Duncan's gang has collected, noting that they're not even fighting hostile tribes, going so far as to want to arrest Duncan for murder. Duncan and his gang kill for a dollar per scalp, and he considers it a hobby.

Duncan gets involved with a plot to rob a train, offering much more profit than he makes off slaughtering Natives. A couple of prostitutes overhear the conversation and try to flee, pursued by the bandits. The Navajo Joe theme starts up as the bandits go after the prostitutes. The bandits find two of their men already dead and Joe takes off after the wagon and the bandits chasing the prostitutes in it.

One of the prostitutes dies of her injuries. The bandits pull off the heist. Esperanza, the town at the center of the action in this, film becomes the stopping point for the now-empty train—empty save for one very effective Indian warrior. He doesn't get a warm reception, but dryly points out to the townspeople that he brought them a train.

He warns the townsfolk that Duncan's men are coming and lets the townspeople know that the money is on the train. The local doctor is in on the heist and gets a bit nervous when he realizes that Duncan's robbery has been foiled. The telegraph lines are cut off and the townspeople have no weapons to defend themselves with. Joe offers to kill the bandits for $1 per head from every person in the town for each kill. They rebuff him, reveal their own racism in the process and send Navajo Joe on his way, probably dismissing the one man who could feasibly take down the bandits. They ill-advisedly send out the doctor to find reinforcements.

The townspeople come to their senses and realize that Joe is the best shot they've got. Joe doesn't doubt that he'll be able to take on the entire gang and he sticks to his price of $1 per head. He also wants the authority of a sheriff. The townspeople ignorantly say that only Americans can be a sheriff, to which Joe points out that his family is American as far back as can be traced, unlike the townspeople's families, and gets himself a sheriff's star.

Joes baits the gang into town with the money, knowing full well that the doctor is working with them, but it doesn't go as planned. This leads to Joe's capture, but not before he takes out quite a few of the thugs. The gang demonstrates their ruthless nature by gunning down innocent townspeople. Joe gets captured when they threaten Estella, the half-Native maid of one of the townspeople played by Machiavelli. The gang practically makes a sport of torturing Joe, but he's rescued by one of the townspeople who, unlike most of them, demonstrates a bit of courage and some very advanced slingshot skills at the same time. Joe gets free and gets back to work.

Joe enlists some help from the townspeople and starts taking down the bandit gang. He takes their horses, leaving them stranded in the town, and the army is on the way. The bandits become increasingly brutal, shooting people to torture others into revealing the location of the money.

Joe gets the bandits on the stolen train by sending them a note letting them know that the money is on it. He appears as they're steaming out of town, and the bandits begin shooting at him wildly. He makes what appears to be a suicide run, eventually—and predictably—taking a bullet from one of the bandits, until they realize that it's not him at all, but one of the bandits that Joe captured and set up. Joe has one more trick up his sleeve, dynamite, and he uses it to take out a good chunk of the bandit horde by blowing up the train.

The bandits pursue him, with Joe taking them out one by one until he faces off against Duncan in the climax, finishing off the last bandit with a thrown hand axe to the head.

## Why Navajo Joe Is Awesome

It's an understatement to say that Native Americans don't get a fair shake in many westerns, but this one is different. Joe is neither not portrayed as a noble savage, nor is he portrayed as some sort of mystical expression of the land itself. He's a man who has been wronged and he also happens to be a very adept fighter.

His fighting style in this film offers something different for western fans accustomed to steely nerved, stand-your-ground type gunslingers. Joe is fast. He uses hit-and-run tactics, stealth and ambushes to win his battles. He doesn't outgun his adversaries; he completely outclasses them. They're just not up to fighting with him.

That said, the film does allow the character to be Native without making him a stereotype. This man is very much connected to the land he lives on and whose family has been on for generations. His fighting skills are very much those that any hunter would likely employ in the same situation. He's patient, and he waits for his target to make mistakes or to wander into his killing field. He's an expert tracker, judging by how easily he manages to catch up with the gang whenever they take off. He's a master of stealth and he's clearly very gifted when it comes to setting up traps for his targets. He uses the greed and racism of the gang to his advantage, playing on them psychologically before attacking them physically.

There's also an interesting element to this film in that the protagonist is Navajo and the antagonist is actually half-Indian. Duncan's harsh upbringing, plagued by racism in its own right, has made him hate essentially everyone. He throws racial epithets at Joe in the climactic scene, ones that could have just as easily been thrown at Duncan's own father.

One of the most refreshing things about Italian westerns is that they're written and directed by people who see the West from an outsider's perspective. They're not caught up in the same old stereotypes that oftentimes manifest in American westerns and that results in some fine storytelling. The characters have depth, no matter what color they are on the surface, and anyone can be a hero or a villain.

Joe stands on his own alongside any of the heroes in this genre. He's as deadly as any gunslinger, as committed to what he's doing as any Mexican revolutionary and as relatable as anyone with his sometimes-superhuman abilities can be. If you find yourself a bit put off by some of the portrayals of Native Americans in American westerns, you might find some relief in this one, because this protagonist is about as memorable as they come.

As just a bonus, when the townspeople get their money back, delivered on the back of Joe's horse, they're surprised that he kept his promise and they rather have their own racism thrown in their faces. One of the townspeople also manages to sum up a lot of the problems with the town in general: "The money's all that matters."

## Appreciating This Spaghetti Western

This is one of the lesser-known spaghetti westerns out there, and that's unfortunate. It's a great film for people who love westerns. It has a unique protagonist who brings something different to the table than shootouts at high noon. It has characters who are complex and interesting and, among the townspeople, the characters are allowed to show that not all of them are bad people and that some of them can even see people for who they are, rather than what they are.

There is plenty of violence in this film and it is graphic, even by the standards of Italian westerns. The fact that Joe manages to get away without a scratch most of the time could be seen as playing on the romantic angle of the Native American who disappears into the landscape like a shadow, but so what? The Man with No Name would have likely died any number of times in any one of the films featuring him, if the director were going for pure realism. Django would have not only likely have had a hard time aiming a gigantic machine gun at street full of bandits, but the heat from it probably would have burned him severely and at least one of those bandits would have been able to shoot him down in the course of the fight. There's no reason that Navajo Joe can't have some rather questionable abilities that allow him to survive as well, and there's no reason to not enjoy it.

The score for this film is by Morricone and it shows. Joe has an appropriately heroic theme, complete with twanging guitars and wildly singing voices. In most films, every time he appeared would probably have been heralded by a soft 4/4 drumbeat and some sense of dread. In this film, the Native has a hero theme and it suits him well.

There's really no way around the fact that this film is a must-see for anyone who loves spaghetti westerns. The music, the filming style and the story are all worth seeing. It's a bit of a departure from the alternately laconic and chillingly cold characters in many of these films. There is an argument to be made, and a good one, that having someone who was fully Native American play the lead would have been better, but this movie is still a huge leap forward for how Native Americans are characterized in westerns. They're so commonly portrayed as the bad guys, the existential threat to not only the characters, but to the progress of civilization itself, that it's easy to forget that they had a civilization that existed long before the arrival of the settlers and that their stories are no less compelling than anyone else's. It's also easy to forget that the cowboys were sometimes the bad guys and that, depending upon which side of a conflict you're on, heroes and villains can switch roles quite easily.

This is one of those films that you'll want to crank up the sound on, because the soundtrack is just as unique as the movie.

## Machine Gun Killers (AKA The Gatling Gun): 1968
## Director:

Paolo Bianchini

**Cast:**

John Ireland

Robert Woods

Ida Galli

This film is also known as *Damned Hot Day of Fire* and *Quel caldo maledetto giorno di fuoco.* It's a historical fiction piece, incorporating Richard Gatling, the inventor of the Gatling—sometimes called Gatlin'—gun. It involves kidnapping, extortion, weapons deals and the Civil War.

**The Plot**

The villain in this film is named Tarpas. The protagonist is Tanner, a Pinkerton Secret Service agent on the Union side. Tarpas is the character who really defines the film, however. He's constantly referred to as a half-breed and the fact that he's an outcast is played up heavily. He's a criminal mastermind, however, and he has connections to powerful people.

Tanner ends up being accused of the crime, and this brings into play another character based on an actual person, Pinkerton. Pinkerton helps Tanner get away so that Tanner can hunt down Tarpas.

At the outset, after a rather confusing scene that is actually shown out of sequence, the Union has decided to look at Gatling's gun, the Civil War being on in earnest, and there's a meeting set up in Las Cruces, New Mexico. On the way, Tarpas's men kidnap Gatling and take the gun.

Tarpas offers the safe return of Gatling for $1 million. He doesn't care whether that money comes from the Union or the Confederacy.

Tarpas is also obsessed with Claudie Lang, a prostitute who he wants to be his wife, but who wants nothing to do with him. Tarpas endures being called a half-breed by just about everyone in this film, and it begins to make it clear why he's such a hard and ruthless man.

Tanner keeps hot on the trail. He eventually manages to seduce Claudie, sending Tarpas into a rage and revealing to Tanner that Tarpas is saying that he plans on getting a $2 million Gatling and his gun, revealing a double-cross. Tarpas gets violent with Claudie, calling her a whore, throwing her around her room, and threatening to kill Tanner.

Tanner has discovered that a member of the commission that was supposedly killed named Ryckert is actually alive and in on the plot. Tanner discovers this after being captured and brutally tortured. Ryckert wants to finish the job and kill Tanner, but Tarpas stops him, wanting to use Tanner as the means of getting the $1 million from the Union side.

Tanner meets with Ryckert and Tarpas's gang, offering them $1 million in diamonds for Gatling's release. The gang appears to release Gatling, but Ryckert sends men after him. Tanner leads the gang away to show them where the diamonds are, not being naive enough to bring them to the meeting.

Tarpas and Tanner get into a fistfight, with Ryckert riding up and gunning down Tanner, Tarpas's gang securing the diamonds for themselves. Tanner, however, was not shot through the heart, as it initially appears, but the hand. This leads to one of the movie's more memorable sequences.

Tarpas and Ryckert go to get their other million dollars, but find that they're not meeting with Bishop, whom they expect, but with Tanner. Tanner guns down Ryckert and gets in a final showdown with Tarpas, first having to get by Tarpas and his Gatling gun and then using the Gatling gun himself.

The film ends with Tarpas turning over the guns, being vindicated and taking off to Washington with the Gatling gun and Mrs. Treble, one of the women he seduces during the film.

## Is It Great or Not?

*Machine Gun Killers* isn't a universal fan favorite with the spaghetti western set, but it has its followers. Quentin Tarantino is said to be a big fan of the film. It does have its moments, but it's not quite as raw or dark as most Italian westerns.

The most interesting character in this film, by far, is Tarpas. He's a villain, to be certain, but he's also sympathetic in a way. He gets no breaks from anyone, constantly enduring racial prejudice and being reminded that he'll never be regarded as anything important.

Tarpas is also dangerous enough that he comes off as the real Big Bad in this film, even though Ryckert is certainly more powerful himself. While the world might think he's gone, the character still wields tremendous power and isn't afraid to use it.

Tanner is an interesting character, but his actions never really have the moral ambiguity that other Italian western protagonists get to play with in their roles. He's after the bad guys, the bad guys are really bad and the situation could get much worse if he fails, given that state-of-the-art military hardware is on the line and a huge conflict is already underway.

Tanner does a lot of womanizing in this film. He's made out to be smoother and more charismatic than the heroes in a lot of these films. It works for this film, but people who are looking for the brooding, plotting and obviously deadly characters won't find it here. Tanner is certainly a dangerous character, but his best action scenes are sometimes spoiled by clichéd direction errors and continuity errors. A six-shooter fires in excess of eight shots in one scene, and then continues to have more in it in another, even though Tanner had no apparent chance to reload. He shoots two men burying him in a shallow grave without really being able to see, his face being covered in a shovelful of dirt. When Tanner gets into it with Tarpas on a wagon, Tarpas is first seen hitting Tanner with the horse reins and then, due to poor editing, is suddenly holding his revolver.

Tanner's escape when he is being beaten up by Bishop's men is also rather howl-worthy. He never really seems to be in danger. Contrasted with other scenes, this might be disappointing for some viewers who are accustomed to the suffering in Italian westerns being very real. For instance, in *The Good, the Bad and the Ugly*, when Blondie gets marched through the desert, it's obvious to the viewer that the character really could die. There's never a sense that Blondie is going to suddenly come around, be totally fine and get away. In *Machine Gun Killers*, there are enough scenes that stretch the suspension of disbelief that it's easy to lose interest for lack of believing that Tanner is really in any danger from anyone.

Does that make the film less enjoyable? In one sense, yes. In other sense, however, it just makes it more of a western adventure film than something one would expect from an Italian western.

## Appreciating This Spaghetti Western
The character that carries this film the most is Tarpas. He's memorable, he's engaging and he seems like the most genuinely dangerous character of the lot. He's not likeable. He's abusive, obsessive, cruel and murderous, but he fits the bill as a great antagonist. He's the best thing about this film, overall.

This film is still fun, however, though it lacks some of the qualities that spaghetti western fans will want to see. The shots aren't anywhere near as artistic or creative as they are in the finest examples of this genre. The action sequences aren't as engaging, and sometimes border on the ridiculous. The dialogue isn't as menacing, either from the protagonist or antagonist.

The story in this film is confusing, so it's likely something that most viewers will want to watch more than once. The film definitely has its moments. Tanner takes a bullet out of his hand in a great scene that gives the film a bit more of an edge than it would have had otherwise.

*Machine Gun Killers* isn't a great film. That much will be obvious to most viewers. It is, however, enjoyable enough to watch and it has some unintentionally funny moments. Some of the editing errors are likely to get a few laughs out of anyone, or make them back up and see if they just saw what they thought they saw. On the other hand, sequences like the kidnapping of Mrs. Treble are very well executed, so this isn't a bad film; it's a film that could have been better, but that's still enjoyable enough as it is.

## Once Upon a Time in the West (1968)
## Director:

Sergio Leone

## Starring

Charles Bronson

Henry Fonda

Claudia Cardinale

*Once Upon a Time in the West* is generally regarded as one of Leone's masterpieces and, outside of the spaghetti western genre, as an example of a great film. It is a long film—epic, really—with a runtime well over 2 hours. The film has all of the trademarks of Leone's direction on display and, despite its long runtime, manages to keep the viewer engaged from start to finish.

## The Plot

*Once Upon a Time in the West* has a rather simple plot, but the scale on which it unfolds makes it into an epic story. The story begins with the assassination of a family of homesteaders and with the arrival of a man who will become known as Harmonica, another nameless, mysterious protagonist, a staple of Leone's.

The family, the McBains, consisted of Brett McBain and his children. Frank had purchased a plot of desert land that, on the surface, looked worthless, but that contained a treasure underneath. There is no other source of water for miles and Frank knew that the railroad, which was fast approaching, would have to have a station there to fill the boilers of the engines. Frank didn't want to buy and sell the land at a bigger price; he wanted to build and run a railroad station.

The men who assassinate the McBains work for the railroad baron Morton, but disguised themselves as members of the Cheyenne gang, led by a man of the same name. Harmonica is confronted by the men when he arrives at a train station, leading to one of the film's most entertaining exchanges before Harmonica guns all of them down.

McBain was married to a woman, Jill, who had not yet arrived at the homestead, but she arrives shortly after the murders. Being his widow, she's now the owner of the land and a fly in the ointment as far as Morton's plans go.

Harmonica meets up with Cheyenne at an inn, saying that he saw three men wearing the same dusters as Cheyenne's gang and that Harmonica himself had put three bullets in them. Cheyenne maintains that they weren't members of his gang.

Peter Fonda plays Frank, the Big Bad in this film. He first attempts to have a hit executed on Jill, but fails because of Harmonica's intervention. There is a race against time in this movie. A clause in the land contract stipulates that Jill has to construct a railroad station before the train tracks reach her land. Cheyenne, Harmonica, and the rest of the gang start pitching in to help her out.

Meanwhile, Frank starts intimidating Jill, first getting her to have sex with him and then making her put the land up for auction. Frank has decided to turn on Morton, buy the land for himself and to buy that land at a ridiculously low price, intimidating all the other bidders at the auction. At the last moment, just before the land sells, Harmonica and Cheyenne show up. Mirroring Tuco and Blondie in *The Good, the Bad and the Ugly*, the two conspire to make it look as if Harmonica is turning in Cheyenne for the bounty on his head, thus getting $5,000, which Harmonica immediately puts forward as a bit on the land, ruining Frank's plan.

Morton does not take Frank's betrayal lightly and pays off Frank's men to kill Frank. Harmonica helps Frank survive, but only does so because he wants to kill Frank himself. Cheyenne's gang manages to kill off Morton's men at the same time. When Frank returns, he heads back to Jill's property to find out who Harmonica is and what Harmonica wants with him.

This sets up the final duel between Harmonica and Frank. Harmonica says that he'll only tell Frank who he is when Frank is about to die. Harmonica manages to win the duel and, while Frank lies dying, the full story is revealed.

Harmonica, when he was young, had an older brother who was killed by Frank and his gang. Frank had forced Harmonica to hold his brother up on his shoulders while his brother was in a noose, hung from an archway. Frank shoved a harmonica in Harmonica's mouth, telling him to "play for your loving brother". Of course, Harmonica eventually tired, letting his brother fall and hang to death. Harmonica has been seeking revenge on Frank since.

Cheyenne and Harmonica leave the property together, but Cheyenne has been mortally wounded since the killing of Morton's men, a fact that he concealed. Slowly expiring of his gut-shot, Cheyenne asks Harmonica to step away while he dies, as he doesn't want Harmonica to see it. The last scenes of the film show Harmonica riding away with Cheyenne's body and the furious construction of Jill's new railroad station.

## Why this Is a Great Film

Right from the start, the viewer is treated to one of Leone's real strengths: his use of sound. In the beginning sequences, with the McBain family, the presence of danger is indicated by the sudden stopping of cicadas as the family prepares a table outside for Jill's arrival. The entire family is massacred, setting up the film as one in which the danger is very real.

As the thugs posing as members of Cheyenne's gang wait for Harmonica to arrive, the soundscape is dominated by the squeaking of a rusty windmill, the desert wind and the sound of flies buzzing. The tension builds, somehow, in a scene that, on the surface, should be boring. Leone was not afraid to stretch a scene beyond all reason and, in fact, this film's best movements usually come when he does so.

By the time the train has unloaded its cargo, the thugs have already positioned themselves for the shootout and we get our first introduction to Harmonica. He plays an eerie tune on the instrument for which he is named. The thugs indicate that they're there to kill him by mentioning that they haven't brought enough horses for all of them—they have three. Harmonica indicates that they brought "two too many."

The gunfight, when it finally comes, is fast and really quite terrifying. Harmonica takes a bullet, but only suffers a minor wound. He guns down all three men with ridiculous ease, slings the arm that was injured by the gunshot and heads off on his way.

Harmonica's leitmotiv is a droning, discordant four-note passage on the harmonica, which he plays by breathing in and out, giving it a remarkably unpleasant sound. It becomes his trademark and becomes a sign that Harmonica is making progress toward his goal, whether that's befriending Cheyenne or killing someone.

This film diverges from the Man with No Name trilogy in that Cheyenne and Harmonica, even though they're habitual lawbreakers, aren't really bad guys. Cheyenne is a bandit, to be sure, but he does seem to have some guiding sense of right and wrong. There seems to be sincerity in his desire to help Jill out—though he does stand to make a profit doing so—and he seems to care about Harmonica as well, beyond what Harmonica can do for him.

Compared to Blondie, Tuco and Angel Eyes, probably the three most famous killers in Leone's films, Harmonica is much more sympathetic. He also can come off as a good guy, even though he is brutal, but his brutality seems more a condition of survival for the world in which he lives rather than a pastime.

Henry Fonda is spectacular in this movie. He's refined, intelligent and completely sadistic and brutal. He's a true psychopath and, to make him even more dangerous, he plays Frank in a way that makes him likeable in a twisted way, if only for the fact that you do not want to be on this guy's bad side. In the sequence where Morton has

Frank's men try to assassinate him, we get a very clear picture of how deadly Frank is. With a little—very little—help from Harmonica, Frank manages to kill several men, many of them at significant range, using only his revolver. Frank hip shoots most of the time. He doesn't need to aim his gun as he basically *is* his gun.

This movie has a higher budget behind it than the films in the Man with No Name trilogy and it does show in the finished product. As Roger Ebert pointed out, there's a lot more background action going on in this film. The towns feel less empty than they did in the Man with No Name trilogy, presumably because there was more of a budget to hire extras and have action going on behind the main characters. This does give the film a somewhat slicker feel than some of Leone's other work, but the director manages to maintain the gritty edge that made him famous. The people in this film might be more numerous, but they still look like they'd benefit from a bath, in many cases. The sets are oftentimes ramshackle-looking affairs, particularly the roadhouse where Harmonica and Cheyenne first meet. There's an omnipresent layer of dirt on just about everything in this film, characters included, and that makes the actors feel more human. They look like they're part of their environments, rather than having the sterile, ultra-contrived look that a lot of today's green-screen productions suffer from.

## Appreciating This Spaghetti Western

This film is essentially the antithesis of most modern films. It's slow, patient and drags scenes out to sometimes grueling length. By the time Harmonica steps in and intervenes in the auction of Jill's land, the sequence has gone on seemingly forever, but the way it resolves is satisfying.

The scene at the beginning of the film, with Harmonica gunning down the three thugs, is a good setup for what the viewer is in for in this movie. One of the thugs lets water drip into his hat and drinks it, with the drip, drip, drip going on forever. A windmill squeaks in the breeze and is shown in detail.

In these films, Leone tends to make every object, every sound into its own world. This lends it a dreamlike quality. When Morton expires in a filthy mud puddle alongside his railroad tracks, we hear the sounds of the ocean that he dreams of reaching with his railroad. It's easy to imagine that he's seeing the little patch of water as an ocean, the rocks as islands. This hyper focus on detail may turn some viewers off, but those who appreciate it will get a good sense of what it would be like to be where the characters are. The rusty whine of the windmill is a common enough sound, but set it in a desert, at a lonely train station and it becomes indicative of the remoteness and primitive nature of the place. This is a place where civilization has not yet reached, but it is coming fast.

There are also some interesting allusions to this era, when robber barons of various sorts tended to run free, buying, selling and sometimes killing to make themselves richer. Morton is told that he's basically a snail who leaves slimy little steel tracks in his wake. Frank tries to be a businessman but he's too rough for that line of work. When he offers Harmonica a $1 profit on the land that Harmonica just bought for $5,000, he says that everyone deserves to make a profit. A businessman would have made the profit more tempting; Frank has gunmen outside in the street waiting to shoot Harmonica down. He might play at being a businessman, but he's still a killer and can't get outside of his own nature.

No one can escape the advancing civilization in this film. Frank cannot escape being a killer. Morton cannot stop himself from trying to take more and more and Harmonica cannot escape the trauma of his past. These men are all animalistic in this regard, driven to do what they do. They affect various levels of refinement—some don't bother—and it's those who just admit what they are who are really the good guys. Jill is an ex-prostitute who wants to build something with what she's inherited and finds the determination and the friends to make that possible. Cheyenne is a bad-boy type, but not evil. He can't help being one of the most notorious bandits out there, however, and he enjoys it, it seems. Harmonica cannot help being a killer, but he accepts it, and that makes him trustworthy somehow.

This film is a bit lighter than the Man with No Name trilogy. The characters aren't quite so ambiguous, but they're still very human and interesting. This spaghetti western is one of the best around. Give yourself an intermission while you're watching it, however, as it's long. Surprisingly, there isn't much fluff, so you'll need to pay attention to the entire film to appreciate it.

http://www.rogerebert.com/reviews/once-upon-a-time-in-the-west-1969

## Day of Anger (1967)
**Director:**

Tonino Valerii

**Starring:**

Lee Van Cleef

Giuliano Gemma

*Day of Anger* features two actors, Gemma and Van Cleef, who will be familiar to anyone who is a fan of the spaghetti western genre. It's a film that puts the cruelty of humanity of full display. Like *The Unforgiven,* which would come decades later, it features a novice gunslinger taking lessons from a pro, but the outcome is much different.

## The Plot
Scott, played by Gemma, is a young man who gets no respect at all from the people of the town he calls home, Clifton. He spends his time cleaning up the streets—literally, not in the sense of taking out criminals—and gets constantly chastised by the people of the town. They're a surly lot and they seem to take out their nasty personalities on Scott almost constantly, telling him to get lost at every opportunity.

Scott dreams of being a gunslinger, however, and passes time admiring the prostitutes at the local brothel, who show him at least some compassion. Scott doesn't know who his mother is and the prostitutes gave him some care.

Then Frank Talby (Van Cleef) rides into town. The man has presence, to say the least, and Scott is immediately taken with him. Talby immediately ingratiates himself to Scott, offering him a dollar to take care of Talby's horse and asking him questions about his life.

Scott and Talby strike up a friendship. Talby encourages the young man, probably for the first time in his life, to have some self-esteem.

Talby, however, is a very deadly man, a bounty hunter, but he soon earns Scott's admiration.

Scott, having taken the name Scott Mary at Talbot's suggestion, teams up with Talby. Talby is hunting down a man named Wild Jack over $50,000, a colossal amount of money at the time.

Eventually, the relationship turns sour. Talby becomes a menace to the town and Scott has to take him on. He does so successfully, proving himself.

## Themes in This Film

Family, friendship and social class are all themes in this film. Despite the fact that this film is not as well known as many of the other spaghetti westerns out there, it does embody much of the best of what this genre has to offer.

The townsfolk are bullies. Poor Scott is treated like trash. He's routinely bullied and psychologically tormented. He's a genuinely nice guy and, while he tries to keep a friendly face, it becomes apparent that it's not because he's a sycophant. He's strong, very strong on the inside.

When a bully decides to try to throw Scott out of the local saloon, Talbot guns him down with impossible quickness, without even getting up out of his chair. After slaying the man, he informs the bartender as to how Talby expects the bartender to testify.

When it comes down to it, Talby is just plain cool, at least at first. He's deadly, capable and intelligent. He's not only capable of gunning down a man in a saloon, but is also capable of getting off the charges based on self-defense. But, in that courtroom, we get the first inkling that Talby has a long, long trail of bodies behind him.

The townsfolk take out their anger at Talby getting off the charges on Scott Mary, which seems to be the local town pastime.

Scott does have one friend, the old stable master who taught Scott to draw. He discourages Scott from embracing a life of violence and tells him that those days are long gone. This man is something of a father figure to Scott or, at least, a wise older friend who tries to make Scott feel less alone.

Talby takes on the role of father, mentor and friend. Right from the start, however, it's not certain whether Talby really wants a friend or whether he just takes a shine to the town outcast because it'll give him an excuse to cut more people down.

Scott proves himself a deadly man, helping Talby to gun down several men who ride into Clifton to take Talby out. Talby, ever the slick outlaw, makes sure that he's not legally accountable for the killing and, in fact, can legitimately say that he defended the marshal against attackers.

Scott is intoxicated with power. He does start to bully his former bullies, but it's hard not to sympathize with him. They had it coming. Talby, corrupt and brutal as he might be, does see something in Scott. The townsfolk ask why Talby made Scott into a rabid wolf, and Talby retorts that Scott was always a wolf; the townspeople made Scott rabid.

## Things Go Awry

Scott takes off after Talby when Talby heads out of town. He tears off across the desert and catches up to Talby. He catches up to join up and persists, even after Talby teaches him a harsh lesson about trust. Scott may be naïve, but he's determined, persistent, and willing to learn.

Talby either sees this in Scott or is amused by it. Either way, the two do end up becoming partners of a sort. Scott follows Talby to a lonely little town where Talby is in the process of calling out Wild Jack. Talby continues to give Scott lessons and starts to show signs that he genuinely likes Scott, deepening Scott's admiration of the gunslinger.

It's not long before it becomes apparent that Talby is going to come into conflict with the people of Clifton, offering Scott something of an opportunity for revenge on his tormentors, but not before he gets beaten senseless once again.

## Harsh Lessons

A lot of this film centers on how people who aren't at all good can appeal to people who actually are good with a few kind words and some kind deeds. Talby gives Scott acceptance. He teaches him lessons along the way, giving each one a number, and shows respect for Scott as he learns them. Given the way the film opens up, it's apparent that Scott really hasn't experienced respect before. After proving that he's reliable and clever—certainly more so than the people of Clifton gave him credit for—Talby helps Scott to pick a pistol, literally putting a dream right in the young man's hand. Scott has earned the respect of Talby and experiences self-respect, something utterly foreign to him.

They soon get to enjoy some well-deserved revenge. Talby means to settle accounts, and does so literally, taking over Wild's bank account after letting the banker know that Talby's aware that he's crooked.

## Things Go Further South

It isn't long before Talby's bullying nature becomes apparent. He's also made a lot of enemies. After all, one does not just walk into a town and take it over based on blackmail and intimidation and expect to be loved.

Murph Short, the old stable master, was also a lawman who got crossways with Talby in the past. He starts pointing out some important facts about Talby to Scott. He says that Talby is getting old and implies that Talby, essentially, is just training Scott to be his gun, given that Talby is slowing down. He points out that Talby did suggest a beautiful gun for Scott, but that it's too long for a gunfighter and that the hammer isn't modified. Between the modified hammer and his skills, Talby can tear off twice the shots that Scott can in the same amount of time.

Scott doesn't believe it and it's hard to blame him. Talby is—as far as Scott believes—the only friend that Scott ever had. Talby renovates the saloon, making it into a rollicking and classy establishment, with plenty of entertainment and even an upscale gambling parlor.

Scott starts to see the truth of what Murph had said, however. Talby may seem like the only friend that Scott had, but he's forgetting Murph. Murph couldn't defend Scott, but he was kind to him and genuinely cared about him. After a deputy is gunned down, Scott turns down an invitation to celebrate, feeling a deep regret at the man's death. "His songs were sad, but he knew how to play," Scott laments, picking up the slain man's harmonica.

It's not long before Scott is being offered another chance to be used and abused, this time by the same people who used to abuse him. Murph is on the side of the townsfolk who want to recruit Scott, but he's not looking to take Scott for a ride. He knows that Talby is bad and he knows how it's all going to turn out. Scott can't just turn on his mentor, however, even if the most honorable man he knows is giving him good reasons to do so.

Of course, the townspeople aren't suddenly good and they plan to off Murph. Scott gets ambushed, but kills his would-be assassin before he can finish the job.

Scott gets shot in his shooting hand but, when a group of thugs are talking about how he's all washed up, he lights a match with a round discharged from his hip at ten paces, making it clear that he's not out of the game at all. He is, unfortunately for him, a notorious legend at this point.

Scott and Talby know they're going to go up against one another. Scott is loyal to Talby, but he's also loyal to Murph. The two old dogs meet in the street when Murph tells Talby to drop his gun belt and, of course, Talby guns him down.

Scott, heartbroken, runs back to the stables and looks in a box that Murph told him to check if anything happened. It contains the gun that Scott needs, modified hammer, right barrel length; it's a gunslinger's tool that Scott, without a doubt, is worthy of in every regard.

Scott demonstrates what he's learned, reciting his lessons from Talby as he takes out Talby's other thugs.

Talby and Scott face off, after Scott has run through every single henchman that Talby can muster. The ending is brutal, to say the least.

## Appreciating This Spaghetti Western

*Day of Anger* might not pop among the most common spaghetti westerns out there, but it's excellent. Van Cleef is particularly good in this role and it gives him a chance to play a hero and an outlaw at once. His portrayal of Talby makes the viewer want to like him. He's not a good guy, but in these movies that's certainly not a reason to dislike someone.

Scott Mary is a great character as well, and goes through quite a transformation. He goes from being a victim of horrible bullying to being a man to be feared in a very short amount of time. He's enamored with Talby, as Talby seems to be the one who has really found out, deep down, what Scott can do. Talby is so slick about it that neither Scott nor the audience sees the game he's playing at first.

Scott is young and strong, both qualities that are desirable in a gunfighter. Scott is willing to learn and learns very quickly, another quality a gunfighter has to have. Scott is also looking for family, something that Talby offers in the form of a mentorship and the appearance of genuine friendship.

Talby is as complex as Scott is. He doesn't seem to take much joy in coming into conflict with Scott and it's hard to believe that he doesn't like Scott at some level. However, that would be the cover that any skilled abuser would use: they really love you, but you're not living up to their expectations.

As was stated earlier, there are some similarities between the narrative in this film and *The Unforgiven*, though they're essentially reversed. Scott wants to learn to be a gunslinger, but he keeps on going long after he's gunned down his first man. He doesn't have the same aversion to killing that the Schofield Kid in *The Unforgiven* does. Talby is the skilled old killer, but he regrets nothing he's done and plans to, essentially, shoot his way into retirement.

This is, however, a film that deals with the consequences of violence and cruelty. Murph is really the mentor that's worth listening to. He doesn't want Scott to get involved with violent men, as Murph has seen enough of them in his time. The killings in this film become increasingly tragic.

When Scott takes out the gang in the final sequences of this film, his style is explosive. He rolls and flips, tosses his gun in the air to reverse his aim and does all kinds of trick shooting, embodying the death that he deals out. One could imagine that Will Munny may have been much the same in his youth: naïve, drunk on power and deadly.

The story in this film is one that's been told many times across many different genres. It still resonates, however, and it's very effectively done here. Part of the fun of this film is seeing Van Cleef, who just happens to be one of the best western villains out there. His cold eyes, sharp features and predator-like demeanor make him perfect for this role.

This film deals with the glamour of the Old West, with all its gunfights and deadly outlaws, and treats them a bit differently. At the end, Scott throws his gun away. It's nice to think that he doesn't go back to being Scott Mary the street sweeper and, of course, he probably can't at that point. It's also nice to think, however, that he really does mean it when he throws his gun away. That he realized that his self-worth doesn't have to come from being able to gun men down and that he doesn't have to become corrupt and a bully to avenge the wrongs done to him. It's nice to think that, but it's also easy to believe that Scott carries on, somehow, because at the point that the film ends, he's already well on his way to accessing a lot of power through his capacity for violence and that's a hard thing to pass up on. Just ask Talby.

## Death Rides a Horse (1967)
**Director:**

Giulio Petroni

**Starring:**

Lee Van Cleef

John Phillip Law

This very dark film stars Lee Van Cleef at his icy, intimidating best. It comes right out of the gate at full speed, not sparing the viewer or giving them any illusions that this film is going to be lighthearted or comedic. It's about death and it starts and stays with that subject from beginning to end, in one way or another.

## The Plot
Bill Meceita has ample reason for revenge. At the beginning of this film, he's a young boy and he watches as his entire family is brutalized by a gang of outlaws. The film spares the viewer nothing in showing this. His mother is raped, his father and sister shot to death and he watches as his family home is burned to the ground in the pouring rain.

By the time the film picks up, Bill is a grown man and one who has obviously been preparing to get revenge for his entire life. He shoots an array of guns, showing that he's far beyond expert with all of them.

Van Cleef, on the other hand—whose character is simply named Ryan—is just getting discharged from a chain gang. He's old, has served 15 years and, though he's obviously had a hard decade and a half, this man is far from broken. When he gets his possessions back, he remembers the 27 bullets that he was arrested with. This man doesn't forget a debt, or a wrong.

It's not long before Ryan guns down his first two victims: two men who were trying to kill him and who sorely underestimated Ryan. The sheriff writes it off as self-defense.

The sheriff notices that the spurs that he took from one of the men that Ryan shot matched the spurs worn by the gang that killed Bill's family. Bill takes off after Ryan after the sheriff tips him off. The sheriff is hesitant to send Bill out on what he knows will be a revenge quest, but he's also been friends with Bill for long enough that he can't hold back the information.

Bill finds Ryan and basically demands to go along with him. Ryan doesn't want to take Bill, saying that Bill has too much hate and that it's going to get Bill killed.

Ryan continues to track down the men he's after, being wonderfully intimidating as he goes. Bill's on the hunt, too, and not far behind Ryan. He establishes himself as a very tough customer when he goes into a saloon, picks a fight by refunding a cheated gambler's money and gunning down several of the thugs. A great example of corrupt law enforcement follows suit, with Cavanaugh, a well-to-do crime boss, getting the sheriff to drop charges against Bill for the killings on the spot. He wants to do business with Bill and, apparently, the local law enforcement does business with Burt Cavanaugh however Burt Cavanaugh sees fit.

Bill soon finds out that Ryan is interested in Cavanaugh as well and warns Bill not to shoot him. Bill doesn't take warnings well, even when they're delivered by someone as intimidating as Ryan.

The two take off after Walcott, the leader of the gang they're both after. Walcott has set himself up in a position of power, but he's planning to take money he's been given by the state to complete public works projects and make it look like a bank robbery. Ryan finds himself framed for the crime, which includes the murder of guards.

Bill catches up to Ryan and breaks him out of jail. The two plot to track down Walcott, with Ryan showing Bill a thing or two about understanding your adversaries enough to know where they're headed next. The two aren't quite friends, however, and Bill tries to leave Ryan behind while he goes off to get Walcott himself. Walcott, as Bill leaves, tells Bill that he wishes he had a son like him.

Bill rides to a mostly abandoned town in the middle of nowhere where Ryan knows that Walcott will bring the stolen money. Bill manages to gun down one of the men who killed his mother, but just as Ryan said, his hate gets the best of him and he gets caught. As he's being tortured, he starts to recognize all the men that were in on killing his family among the bandits.

Ryan gives Bill a hard time about getting caught when he rescues him and the townsfolk, grateful to have anyone stand up to the bandits that have been victimizing them, free Bill.

Ryan, Bill and the villagers prepare the village for a siege by the bandits, and they do it very well under Bill's direction. The bandits lose many men in their charge, enough to make them hold off actually entering the village the day they come back.

Bill finds out what the audience already likely knows—Ryan was tied to the murder of Bill's parents. The two make peace and take out the gang in a long, tense and wonderfully staged battle. In the end, the two face off, Ryan feeling like he probably deserves to die, not even having a round in his gun to face Bill with and refusing to defend himself. Bill forgives Ryan, as much as he can, and the two part ways.

## Worth Watching

This film did not get universally good reviews when it came out, but it has good reviews on some of the larger film websites today. There's good reason for the latter, but the former is hard to figure out.

On the surface, as some critics suggested, this is a pretty conventional western plot. One protagonist, Bill, survived his family being murdered by outlaws and is forever scarred, understandably, by that experience. The other protagonist, Ryan, has been double-crossed by the same outlaws and wants revenge, and money. This is pretty conventional plotting for a western, on the whole. The film, however, doesn't end up being so much about the plot that it starts out with.

During the second half of the movie Ryan and Bill start to respect one another. Ryan helps Bill more than he really needs to and Bill returns the favor. When Ryan doesn't want to help Bill, it seems not because he wants to sabotage him, but protect him in some regard. Even at first, Ryan warns Bill about having too much hate in his heart.

It's curious why he doesn't just shoot Bill instead of more or less inconveniencing him. He says he doesn't want Bill with him. Ryan seems good at getting rid of people he doesn't want around, and Bill would be easy prey for him.

There's the obvious old-gunslinger and new-gunslinger convention here. This formula still works. *The Unforgiven*, one of the most popular and highly regarded films in this genre, uses this trope, and it works. It works in *Death Rides a Horse*, as well. There are scenes where Bill is ready to tear off after the bad guys, but has no idea, really, what he's doing, and it's obvious. Ryan, in some scenes, almost like a professor of Outlaw 101, explains how the outlaws are going to do things to Bill, giving Bill an edge he wouldn't have otherwise. It's a very teacher-and-student relationship, and paternal.

Both of these characters are extremely dangerous men, but in very different ways. Van Cleef is great at portraying what makes Ryan deadly. He's just ten steps ahead of you, no matter what you have in mind. He has seen it all and he has been so intimidated in his life, in all likelihood, that you can't intimidate him any longer. He's not a cold character—this isn't an Angel Eyes clone—but he's a steady character. He doesn't flinch. He starts his day by shaving, figuring out what to do next and he gets it done.

Bill is incredibly fast with a gun. Whether or not this film is conventional in his motivation, Law seems to put a bit more into it than he had to. The character comes off as desperately wanting to save his family as much as he wants to avenge them. When he sees the people involved in the murders, he flashes back to the incident— a red-tinged, chaotic version of it—and relives the terror and the rage he felt when it was happening. Each of the men on whom he takes out his vengeance almost seems like a chance for him to rewrite the book, as it were, and to change how the situation ended. The present-day Bill probably would have gunned down all the men that killed his family, but he was a child at the time, and there was nothing to be done…yet.

This movie is good. It's not the best spaghetti western of the lot nor is it the best movie ever made, but it's a lot better than many other movies that get plenty of praise in any genre.

Watching Van Cleef in this movie is great. He's excellent in roles where he plays the past-his-prime—or so you thought—gunslinger who's got a lot of villainy in him. In this role, however, he gets to be the good version of that character. He was tied to the murder of Bill's family but, like Bill, he couldn't do anything to stop it, simply because he showed up too late. Like Bill, he would have stopped it if he could.

Ryan starts to think of, and even calls Bill, his son by the end of the movie. There's $1 million in public works funds being hijacked in this movie. If one pays attention to the story, the money actually becomes something of an afterthought.

## Appreciating This Spaghetti Western

This movie has a Morricone score, so the music is worth listening to, even if you were to skip this spaghetti western. You should not skip this one, however.

The acting in this film is good. In fact, it's better than a lot of the acting that you'll see in these films. The giants in this genre are generally very well-acted affairs, but westerns can get away with stock characters, clichéd lines and bad attempts at humor and be forgiven. This film doesn't need to ask for forgiveness on any of those grounds. When Van Cleef uses the standard "settle accounts" line, it doesn't come off as a cliché. His performance is good enough that you believe he should be talking that way.

This movie doesn't come off as an act. Law manages to put the gunslinger hero hat on here and there, but his performance has enough subtlety to it that you can tell it's all surface. Maybe it was intentional or maybe it was because a lot of what's required to act in a western, such as being able to ride a horse, were things that Law didn't even know how to do before shooting this film. His gunslinger act feels like an act, as it should. Bill is not a force for justice and vengeance. He's scarred; deeply so and to the extent that his bravado is nearly suicidal at times.

This film has many fans among those who love the spaghetti western genre. Judging by the writing out there about this film, most people who see it like it. Quentin Tarantino has used the flashback effect in his own films.

There were reviews written about this film that were downright vicious when it came out. In retrospect, it's hard to say why. This film has some flaws to it, to be sure, and it's probably not going to appeal to every viewer out there. The same could be said of any film.

*Death Rides a Horse* is in the public domain, which means that you can go to any site where it's available and stream it, legally, and see for yourself. Italian westerns and public domain films have a reputation—fair or not—as being low-budget, bad films that no one really wants to see. There are other films that are vital to their genres and that have influences that vastly outsize their budgets and their popularity in the public domain. *Night of the Living Dead*, for instance, is in the public domain, so don't let being a free movie make you think this isn't a good movie.

Like the aforementioned film that's also in the public domain, *Death Ride a Horse* didn't get pegged for being as good as it really is in its time, at least not by all critics. Over time, it's becomes a respected film. Anyone who loves the Italian western genre should watch it. It will be time well spent and both actors give great performances in this movie. Again, this film is long, coming in at nearly two hours, but it's worth the time investment, for certain.

## The Great Silence (1968)
## Director:

Sergio Corbucci

## Starring:

Klaus Kinski

Jean-Louis Trintignant

*The Great Silence* is a film with two endings. The original ending is so dark that the filmmakers were forced to shoot an entirely other ending to the film for some markets. It's also unusual in terms of its setting and in its portrayal of bounty hunters and the law in the Old West.

## The Plot

Set in the mountains of Utah in 1899, the first variation on the norm for westerns with which *The Great Silence* presents the viewer is the stark and wintery landscape rather than an endless desert. The snow-choked forests provide the stage for this drama, and they are just as unforgiving as the rest of the story will turn out.

Silence is the first major character introduced to the viewer. He guns down a group of bounty hunters, who are in pursuit of the film's main protagonists, a group of impoverished and desperate settlers who are forced into banditry to survive. He carries a Mauser C96, an advanced pistol for the time, which he carries in a distinctive wooden holster.

We learn that Silence hates bounty hunters and hunts them himself. Like the antagonists in this film, he does his killing without crossing over into outright murder. He makes sure that whomever he shoots draws first, making it self-defense.

The settlers have bounties on their heads. They really haven't any choice but turn to thievery, as there is nothing for them to eat and the weather is unrelentingly cold and brutal. They even turn to stealing horses for food. The prices on their heads have drawn a group of bounty hunters to Snowhill, who seek out the settlers as, essentially, easy cash.

Klaus Kinsky plays Loco, the most ruthless and cruel of the bounty hunters. He's also very good at what he does. Like Silence, he never murders. He always makes sure that whatever he does is on the right side of the law, but seems to truly enjoy the killing he does.

Loco eventually kills a man whose wife, Pauline, hires Silence to avenge. In the meantime, a new sheriff, Burnett, has arrived in town, being dispatched by the governor to deal with the culture of bounty hunting and the miserable conditions in Snowhill. Burnett regarded the mission as largely hopeless, given the size of the area he'd have to patrol and the conditions due to the brutal weather.

Burnett immediately tries to impose law and order on the town, but quickly finds out that the bounty hunters and the local justice of the peace are well versed in using the law to their advantage and that they have a vested interest in the bounty hunting in Snowhill.

Pauline and Silence start to fall for one another. The sheriff ends up falling prey to Loco along the way. The big showdown at the end of the film comes, and it ends in a way that the viewer is not likely to see coming.

## The Great Darkness
*Don't read further if you haven't seen the movie. You've been warned.*

This is a very political western. The basic premise of the film is born out in how the characters regard and are regarded by the law.

Silence hates bounty hunters. He's on a personal mission. What he wants to do is kill them, technically making him a murderer, whether or not his motives are sympathetic. Silence, however, has figured out how to make the law work for him. He's a very fast, accurate shooter and he uses a very advanced firearm that carries more rounds than the six-shooters just about everyone else is carrying. This allows him to let the bounty hunters draw first, relying on his skill and weapon to give him a fully legal kill. He's figured out how to murder for revenge the legal way.

Loco is a brutal, cruel and psychopathic man. He's clearly motivated by money, but seems to enjoy the killing a bit more. He's a formidable foe and has absolutely no qualms about whom he kills or how he kills them. He's practically a lawyer. He understands the law well enough to make sure that he can murder and get away with it, and oftentimes collect a reward from it. He's figured out how to turn murder into a legal, capitalist enterprise.

Pollicut is the justice of the peace. He's corrupt and involved in the murdering himself, but his corruption is more of an antagonistic force in the film than is his murderous nature. He's made an industry of his own corruption and callousness, and he has tremendous power.

Sheriff Burnett is the most human character in the mix. He's a lawman and he wants to get the bandits amnesty, given that any human being in their desperate situation would have to resort to desperate measures to survive. He's a good guy, a very good guy. Of course, he dies.

In fact, the most cynical thing about this movie is its ending, though it's generally cynical all the way through. The way that Loco, Pollicut and the bounty hunters take the word of the law and pervert its intent would make any evil genius proud.

### The Industry of Evil

This film is built around a very disturbing premise. The bounty hunters in this film are oftentimes referred to as "bounty killers." That's really what they are. The basic premise regarding bounty hunters in most films is that they'd rather bring someone back alive, if possible. This is even used as a narrative device, forcing a bounty hunter to spare the life of a villain and, of course, putting the bounty hunter in danger because of that. In this film, the bounty hunters seem to prefer to kill the people they're after. They've developed such an effective system of doing so without being held accountable that it's obvious that this is the case. They like the killing and the reward, not just the reward.

There's an entire industry built up around the number of wanted people near Showhill. Pollicut, the justice of the peace, is in on it, setting up a situation where the industry has corrupted the legal system. Burnett tries to take this on as best he can, but it's too much for one man to change.

That applies to Silence, as well. He's clearly someone to be taken seriously, and he's every bit the spaghetti western protagonist. He's not only a man of few words; the character is actually mute. The bounty killers in Snowhill, however, are too much for him as well, and he eventually falls to Loco. This comes as something of a shock, as Silence is set up as a character that might go on to figure in other films. He has all the qualities required for an enduring spaghetti western hero: signature weapon; strong but silent; murderous, but for good reasons; and he's more dangerous than the average villain.

Loco turns out to be an unstoppable force in this film. He doesn't even shoot the poor sheriff; he shots the ice under his feet, sending him to his death in the icy lake. Of course, this means that no one can say that he shot the sheriff. Loco is that careful and, at least according to the general outline of the law in this film, if not according to 1899 Utah law, Loco never breaks the law. Not once. Everything Loco does is within the realm of the legal, and he murders many people throughout the course of this film.

The ending is the most shocking part of this film. The gunning down of the settlers, while they are totally helpless and hostage, is brutal. The bounty hunters don't flinch before doing it, but it's certain to make the audience flinch. It's hard to watch and, in fact, by the end of this film, every likeable character is dead. It's not easy to take and it's easy to believe that it wouldn't have made it into an American western.

## Appreciating This Spaghetti Western

This is one of the darkest spaghetti westerns you'll find, possibly even the darkest. It takes the time to make you care about the protagonists and to despise the antagonist. It takes the time to get you involved in their stories as well as how they relate to one another. Then, it does exactly the worst thing possible with the trust you placed in it, and it betrays you utterly.

This film has been called among the most political westerns out there, as well, and it was succeeded by two other films, *The Mercenary* and *Companeros*, by the same director that were also regarded as quite political.

In this film, the politics are clear enough. The common people are being ignored and brutalized by the government. A capitalist industry has sprouted up based on harvesting the regular people for cash. The law sets up an impossible situation, turning the people into criminals. It then puts a price on their heads in reaction to their crimes, all according to the law. An industry springs up made up of men who have no compunction about killing for money, and corruption allows those involved in the legal system to profit off of the entire enterprise, along with the bounty killers. Everyone follows the law—wink, wink, nudge, nudge—and manages to get away with everything the law is supposed to prevent, at the same time.

The film is a frightening one in many regards. The people who have bounties on their heads in this film are walking murder victims. The bounty hunters don't want to bring them in alive and it's a scary thought. It takes a very common western trope—bad people get prices on their heads—and turns it completely upside down. The bounty hunters in this film are thoroughly evil.

If you're looking for something that lets you stare into the abyss long enough for it to stare back into you, *The Great Silence* just might fit the bill. It's a very well acted film. The recent DVD release is good quality and contains an alternate ending to the film that's much happier, but which also sort of removes the film's most memorable part.

The sound on most of the releases of this film is not excellent and there are some obvious low-budget touches. It makes it work better. With the exception of *Once Upon a Time in the West*, most of the best spaghetti westerns are low-budget and make the most of the story they have to make up for the sparse sets and other production limitations. This film follows in that tradition. The characters, the premise and the way that the setting is shot all make this a great film, and the ending is something that most people will not forget.

## Viva Django (AKA Prepare a Coffin): 1968
**Director:**

Ferdinando Baldi

**Starring:**

Terence Hill

Jose Torres

If you're looking for direct connections to *Django*, *Viva Django* is likely to be a bit vexing. It stars Terence Hill as the title character in place of Franco Nero. The film also plays with the canon chronology established in *Django*, so the viewer needs to have some flexibility with the character, the story and the larger story of Django's life when watching this. Terence Hill looks enough like a younger Django to be convincing, but he wouldn't come into his own as a star until the *Trinity* franchise was released years later.

### The Plot
Horst Frank is a crooked politician. Django works for him as an escort transporting gold. Django wants out of the life he's made and wants to move to California. Frank doesn't want Django to go, offering Django influence and riches if he sticks with the politician. Django tells his frenemy that he's headed out with a large quantity of gold in the morning, along with his wife. Of course, it doesn't go well.

Django and his wife get ambushed—Frank's behind it—and Django's wife gets killed. Django takes several bullets himself and the thugs manage to rob the shipment of gold, Frank looking on with approval. Django buries his wife and, since he's got his riding coat and hat on at this point, his trademark costume, it's obvious that someone's going to pay for killing Django's wife, and pay dearly.

Django has a rather elaborate plan in this film. He apparently disappears for a while and starts working as a hangman. Anyone who is slated to be hanged by Django, however, might get a lucky break instead of a broken neck. He's saving some of the criminals he's supposed to hang and building up a posse to help get revenge on Frank. Django not only saves the men's lives, he gives them the money that Django himself was supposed to earn for performing the hanging. He lets the people he saves know, however, that they are between a rock and a hard place and it's either head off to join with the others that Django's saved or just end up getting hung again or being on the run forever.

Django is clever; he uses an apparatus with a hook to make it look like the condemned men have been hanged. It's an effective magic trick, and one that Django obviously has down pat by the time the movie picks up and shows him at his new enterprise.

Django's offer to the men is simple. They help him settle his account and he helps them get vindicated. Django will make sure that they get to find the people who falsely accused them and get them to recant. Just to make sure they understand, Django guns down three men who decide they want to leave the enterprise, with help from the last man he saved, Garcia, a Mexican character who has serious knife throwing skills.

The gang goes out and terrorizes the false witnesses. Django forbids them to kill any of the witnesses, as the men he's saved are not murderers and murder would obviously just send them to another hangman. They have a good time pretending to be phantoms, however, riding up to their accusers' houses in a wild band, beating and otherwise brutalizing them and warning them to go back and recant.

Garcia, however, turns out not be the best sort of solider to have in your private army. As Django heads off to save Garcia's wife, Mercedes, from being hung herself, Garcia plots to double-cross Django and get a shipment of gold for themselves. Django wants them to capture the members of the Lucas gang who are planning to rob the gold and bring the Lucas gang in. Garcia offers his alternate plan to Django's posse and shoots two men who refuse to go along.

The gang betrays Django and Django gets caught and brutally tortured by Lucas's gang. Frank comes into play, turning out to be behind Lucas's gang. Django's gang may have betrayed Django, but they've also made some powerful enemies in the process.

Interestingly, for a man on the run from his past and trying to keep a low profile, Django hasn't started using an assumed name and Frank recognizes who he is as soon as Lucas tells Frank that Django has been captured. Mercedes and the Justice of the Peace keep an eye on things from afar, not really doing much, but seeing what they might be able to do to help their friend Django.

Django's friends manage to rescue him. Django decides he needs some dynamite, so things are going to get good.

Frank sets himself up as the absolute power behind Lucas's gang, needing the gang to continue his corrupt enterprises but not wanting the gang to bungle anything anymore. Django sets out to disrupt the gang, but his posse now consists of one very brave, very loyal but also very old man. The two pull it off, however, and Lucas dies a horrible death in retribution for what he did to Django's wife.

Meanwhile, Garcia proves that he's a first-class scoundrel. He seems to part ways amicably with the rest of the gang, saying he wants to get his family and getting a very generous share of the gold from the gang as he parts. The gang might have betrayed Django, but they're not evil, except for Garcia, who plunges further down the spiral into villainy in one of the movie's many betrayals.

Mercedes seems to have some sort of a psychic bond with her husband and she desperately wants Django to let him live. Django doesn't necessarily want to kill Garcia, but he wants the gold they were supposed to have stolen so Django can finish out his revenge on Frank.

Django, along with the help of Garcia and Mercedes, gets Frank to go meet Django in a cemetery. Anyone who knows Django already knows how that situation is likely to go down for people who have an account that Django intends to settle.

Django manages to pull the coffin trick one more time at the end of this film and it's incredibly satisfying. Few people have it coming as much as Frank does and Django settles the account for good.

## Django as a Hero

Django is a very popular character with spaghetti western fans. The fact that Tarantino named his own spaghetti western tribute after this character is an indication of that. He's a lot different from many of the protagonists in these films.

When the Man with No Name intervenes to help someone who's helpless or shows a bit of compassion, it's always surprise. It's a reminder that he's human and that he has a heart and a sense of right and wrong. Django, on the other hand, has an obvious sense of right and wrong. It's not surprising when he goes to save Mercedes from being hung, because he's that kind of person, at the heart of it.

Django is a lethal man. He's fast with his gun, he's very smart and he knows how to outwit adversaries. These are things he has in common with the protagonists of Leone movies, who are often long-term chess players who don't mind drawing out their plans for months, years or even a lifetime. What Django doesn't have in common with those characters is his motivation.

In this film, he's motivated by redressing a wrong, just as he is in the original film. He'll risk his life to do what's right and to make sure that accounts are settled, as he puts it. This puts him somewhere between the traditional western hero and the spaghetti western protagonist. Django can certainly cross into morally ambiguous behavior now and then, and he's actually at his best when he does, but those moments tend to be different from those where other spaghetti western heroes do the same.

When Django crosses a legal or ethical line, it's to even things out. Revenge might be personal to him, but it's revenge that anyone could understand, really. Someone kills his wife, Django kills that person. Someone betrays Django's trust or turns out to be simply murderous and dishonorable, Django kills that person. Django doesn't do it for gold or power. In fact, he seems to be a bit repulsed by those who wielded power over others for unfair and unjust reasons.

Django is a dark character, and showing up in graveyards is something of a trademark for him, but he's dark in a good way. The Man with No Name would give you money and send you out of town under the cover of night to make sure you and your family weren't victimized by a group of gangsters. Django would probably give your family the money and escort you all to the next town, killing anyone who tried to take advantage of you. In this regard, Django is a very likeable character. He's truly a good guy, but he's definitely a chaotic sort, not caring much for the law or those who are in power. Oftentimes, he acts on the notion that the only way to make things right is to subvert the law and, if necessary, take out the corrupt people behind its excesses.

In this film, Django really doesn't kick into high gear until the last third of the story, but it's a great burst of spaghetti western violence when he does. Seeing a torch fly in through the windows and set the drapes on fire, Frank yells, "That must be him!" It is, and it's on.

## Appreciating This Spaghetti Western

This spaghetti western comes later, during the heyday of the genre, and it shows. The elements that made the first films in this genre stand out so much are all very developed here. Django is incredibly fast and dangerous, but he's human and you can believe that he's in danger. It's feasible for a hero not to live through one of these films.

Django also crosses the ambiguity line when he assembles a gang of private soldiers by freeing them from their death sentences. He's not a lawman and he's not above using the law for his own gain in this regard. That makes him a lot more fun than the always upstanding types with their white hats and freshly washed horses. Django looks like he lives on the frontier and so does everyone else around him, so there is that spaghetti western element of realism to the character that really makes him work.

Terrence Hill would go on to become the star of the *Trinity* films, which were essentially parodies of spaghetti westerns. In this role, Hill is really quite good as the title character. He's surprisingly dark and brooding and he looks a lot like Franco Nero, so it's not jarring to see someone else play this role.

Garcia is a great villain. The character doesn't get much screen time to develop a lot of complexity, but the writers made the most of what he's given. At first, he seems just plain evil but, toward the end, we start to see him for who he is. He's not really looking to get rich so much as he's looking not to be desperately poor. His wife loves him dearly, despite the fact that he's very ruthless at times, but he sticks with Django at the end and redeems himself as much as anyone could.

This film is also classic in terms of the genre, in that you have to wait until the end, or close to it, for the real payoff. When it does come, however, it's the sort of thing that would likely send a fan of this genre out of their seat cheering. It's very well executed and it gives Django fans a chance to see him with his trademark weapon and tactic one more time, making this a great way to bring the character back to the screen.

This film doesn't get a lot of praise for being a particularly innovative spaghetti western, but that's what makes it enjoyable. Not every sci-fi movie is *Star Wars* or *Alien*, but there are plenty of other ones out there that are great films without being genre definers or innovators. Not every thriller is *Rear Window* or *The Usual Suspects*, but plenty of them are downright thrilling, even if they're not particularly inventive.

*Viva Django* will give you exactly what you want if you're into Italian westerns. It's violent, dark, and sometimes funny in a sardonic way, and it's built around a classic tale of revenge and betrayal. It has the bizarre elements that spaghetti western fans will like, but rather than an extended host of people staring at one another this film's bizarreness is in its being at once connected with and at the same time completely disconnected with the other Django films. You'll get your Django, but don't expect the plot to start and stop like part of a trilogy. In this regard, Django is somewhat like the Man with No Name. It's obviously the same character, but also it's not, so the viewer has to give some ground here.

It's worth it to give that ground. This isn't a great, brilliant and genre-defining Italian western, but it's a very good one. It's a lot of fun and it's worth seeing.

# The Grand Duel, AKA Storm Rider: 1972
## Director:

Giancarlo Santi

## Starring:

Lee Van Cleef

This 1972 spaghetti western was directed by the man who assisted Leone on the production of *The Good, the Bad and the Ugly*. It stars Lee Van Cleef as a tough, smart sheriff with the requisite cold stare and fast guns. As far as spaghetti westerns go, it's not the best of the lot, but it definitely has enough of the trademarks of this genre to keep a fan happy.

## The Plot

Van Cleef plays Clayton, a sheriff who is the guy no one in their right mind would want to mess with in this film. He establishes his steel nerves by slow walking down a street where bounty hunters and a man with a very high price on his head, Wermeer, seem destined to have a shootout. Surprisingly for a lawman, Clayton reveals the position of each of the bounty hunters to the wanted man as he makes his way down the street, giving the outlaw the advantage.

Wermeer shoots his way out of the trap, but the action in this sequence is more along the lines of a kung fu movie than a standard western, with Wermeer literally launching himself over a roof using a wagon as a fulcrum.

Clayton tries to trick the bounty hunters by faking shooting Wermeer, but they get caught out and end up getting in a gunfight. The two make it out of town, rendezvousing and heading to Silver Bells.

Clayton isn't after the bounty, but he intends to get Wermeer to Saxon. The bounty hunters remain in pursuit. Things aren't what they appear, however, and the bounty hunters aren't just after the bounty and Clayton isn't involved in this to catch an apparent bad guy. He knows that Wermeer is innocent of the charges against him and he means to prove it.

The bounty hunters eventually catch up to Wermeer, and beat and torture him until Clayton frees him.

The two head off to Saxon City to confront the Saxon brothers. Wermeer is accused of killing their father, but he didn't commit the crime. The brothers offer Clayton a huge sum of money if he and Wermeer leave town. The charge is fraudulent and the conflict is entirely based in sharing the wealth from a silver mine, which Wermeer's father refused to do, leading to him being killed.

After passing up an offer to have the charges dropped, Wermeer is slated to be hanged. Clayton is actually the killer and, after having revealed as much, he prepares to duel with the Saxons.

Clayton ends up winning the duel and goes back to being a sheriff. Wermeer ends up not wanting the silver, escaping to Mexico.

## Not a Bad Time

While this film may have a Leone connection, it's not a Leone film and does lack his particular genius. It's a fairly standard spaghetti western with a falsely accused man and a family of thugs that rule a mining town with an iron fist. As such, the Saxons are serviceable, with Adam Saxon being a particularly odd character. If Adam had appeared in a film set a hundred years earlier, he may have been described as a foppish dandy sort, though he's a sadistic killer underneath it all, gunning down a poor old drunk in the middle of the street and knowing full well that his victim didn't have a chance in the fight.

Van Cleef is good, as always, though this role doesn't give him as much of a chance to show off his chops as do others. His character in this film is rather stock: the conflicted, tough sheriff who sometimes crosses to the wrong side of the law.

*The Grand Duel* definitely does have its moments. A night sequence detailing a showdown between the Wermeer and Saxon clans is particularly eerie, with steam obscuring the camera's field of view and a fast shootout taking place without what happened being made readily apparent.

During the second half of the film, it becomes more of a mystery than a chase film, with Wermeer and the Saxons trying to figure out who gunned down old man Saxon.

When Clayton gets into town, he immediately asserts himself as someone not to be tangled with. When someone tries to keep him out of the bar, Clayton just gut-punches him and tosses him aside, walking into a bar and having it out with the marshal.

When Clayton does get his best scenes, Van Cleef's abilities shine. He's great at being indifferent, sardonic and calm in the face of danger, even if it happens to include a gun being stuck in his face.

Van Cleef, of course, is as good as ever in the gunfight scenes. The director attempted to mirror Leone's style in these fights, with long shots of the fighter's eyes, plenty of silence and people gunning one another down with impossible speed, given that they're using single-action revolvers. Nonetheless, the scenes are exciting enough and it's always enjoyable to see Van Cleef take out a host of gunslingers without breaking a sweat.

## Appreciating This Spaghetti Western
*The Grand Duel* isn't a great spaghetti western, but it's likely to go down well with those who love the genre.

The direction in this film is not at the level of Leone. The story wanders at times, the dialogue and scenarios tend to be repetitive and the villains are far less intimidating than they are in other films of this genre. Some of the action is very over the top, breaking from the standard in many of these films where the violence is visceral and sometime downright terrifying.

*The Grand Duel,* however, does have enough of the spaghetti western feel to be a lot of fun and is best watched with that in mind. This isn't going to stay with you the way that some of the best spaghetti westerns will, but it's a good time and, despite its shortcomings, is enjoyable enough to watch.

## The Legacy and Influence

The films featured in the following sections are not spaghetti westerns, but show a great deal of influence from that genre. Two of the films are Eastwood films, both of which show him drawing on his spaghetti western characters and expanding upon them, in fact, creating something wholly new but also rooted in his past performances. The tough, effective man of few words is still very much present in his performances in these films, but it's more nuanced and more his own.

Other films, such as *Django Unchained*, are direct tributes to these films, oftentimes taking the best of what spaghetti westerns have to offer and making them even better. *Dead Man*, a surreal western shot in black and white did not get great reviews but, much like the spaghetti westerns from the previous section of this book, it is complex, sometimes hard to follow and very dark.

Spaghetti westerns oftentimes capitalized on American legends about the West and portrayed them in ways that made the violence more real and consequential. In films such as *The Unforgiven*, the audience sees that expanded upon, with sorrow replacing the sense of righteous vengeance and murder cast in a light that's far more appropriate, given the finality of the act and the scars that it leaves. Watch these films and appreciate them for what they are, but realize how much they owe to the Italian reinvention of the western genre.

## The Wild Bunch (1969)
**Director:**

Sam Peckinpah

**Starring:**

Ernest Borgnine

William Holden

All good things must come to an end, even the Old West. That is what *The Wild Bunch* is really about. Remarkable for its graphic violence, truly murderous protagonists and the early 20th century period in which it is set, this epic-scale western is part of the National Film Registry and among the most beloved westerns of all time.

## The Plot

Peckinpah starts us out with a violent story from the first minutes of this film. It follows a gang of outlaws led by a man named Pike who are far past their prime. During the first sequence of the movie, they lose a significant amount of their crew to a gang of bounty hunters hired by a railroad who foil the gang's attempt to rob a railroad office of silver.

The robbery is a bust, with the silver actually being a load of steel washers. The gang decides to head to Mexico after meeting up with an old associate, Sykes. One of the men, Angel, is from Mexico and they head back to his home village to cool off and figure out what they're going to do next.

It's not long before they're involved in another crime: a train heist of military weapons. The village is the operating base of a Mexican federal general named  Mapache who lords over it like his personal fiefdom. Angel isn't having it and, after shooting one of the general's lovers, makes a powerful enemy. Mapache, the general, is the one offering the gang gold for the robbery, so he holds off on getting revenge on Angel.

Angel, however, happens to be sympathetic to the Revolution and wants to give a case of rifles to the people fighting against Mapache's tyranny. The gang agrees to let Angel take one of the 16 crates of rifles to the revolutionaries, but he gives up his share of the gold from the job in exchange.

The railroad has not given up on finding the gang and Deke, a convict who knows the gang and who has been released from prison in Yuma to go after them, pursues them across the border. The train is full of military weapons and soldiers, but Deke is the only one of their total number who is at all competent. The gang easily robs the train, takes off with the guns and forces Deke to go after them into the Mexican desert. The gang buys time by blowing up the bridge into Mexico, nearly killing Deke's men and sending the lot of them into the Rio Grande.

Mapache is not to be trusted, of course, and the gang delivers the crates of guns to him one by one, not giving him a chance to kill them before they get their money. Mapache learns that Angel has given guns to the revolutionaries and manages to capture him. The gang is helpless to take on the entire group of soldiers at the village and Angel is brutally tortured by the general and his men.

The gang, however, cannot bear it and return to try to free Angel. It doesn't go well, resulting in a shootout with the general's troops. Among the stolen guns was a machine gun, which Pike and Engstrom, played by Ernest Borgnine, manage to massacre most of the soldiers with before being killed themselves.

Deke shows up and lets his incompetent bounty hunter crew take the bodies of the men back to the U.S. for the reward, knowing that the U.S. Army will kill them before they ever get there, as the bounty hunters opened fire on the Army soldiers during the bridge incident. Sykes turns out to have survived and hooked up with the revolutionaries. He invites Deke to go along; Deke accepts the offer, not wanting to go back to prison or get killed, and they ride off, the last two outlaws of a truly wild gang and among the last of the Old West altogether.

## The Brutality of It All

The violence in this film is graphic and, at first blush, that may make it seem like that's what makes it stands out. There's more to it than that, however.

The gang in this film is murderous through and through. They are hardened killers, experienced thieves and absolutely the definition of outlaws. They care for nothing but their own chances of making a profit and even the most significant friendships, between Pike and Engstrom, feel like they could end in a hail of lead at the slightest provocation. These are not nice men. They are not misunderstood heroes who are oppressed by the law. They are, in every sense of the word, criminals, and they are exceptionally violent ones that that. This film does not celebrate them for that fact, but it doesn't cover its eyes when they open up with a revolver, a shotgun or even a machine gun, either.

In this regard, this film does not glamorize the Old West outlaw, but it does show some nostalgia for such characters. These are the last of the lot, really, and their way of life is quickly evaporating before them. Trains make it possible to cross the country fast and there are fewer remote places for them to hide. The law is everywhere, whether it's the real law or the law for hire in the form of bounty hunters. Head south and Mexico is changing, too, and going there means being caught up in a revolution that is bloody to the hilt and that is full of players who will double-cross a gringo as soon as they can, and as brutally as they can, it seems. These men, the wild bunch, are artifacts of a time that is quickly passing into history and one sees this not only in the story, but in the items that play a part in the story.

## A Preview of Things to Come

One of the criticisms that you'll likely see made of this film is some nitpicking about the machine gun, which plays a significant part at the end of the film. The film is set in 1913 and the machine gun is a Browning M1917, which, as you may have guessed from the name, had not been designed at that time. In the context of this film, this isn't important. The machine gun, for all the carnage that it causes, is symbolic more than realistic.

The gang in this film carries revolvers, but they also carry Colt 1911 pistols, a semi-automatic that is still in widespread use and that was a huge innovation for the time. A German military officer who is working with Mapache wants the gang to get access to American military weapons for him, for obvious—and sinister, given that

World War I was right around the corner—purposes. In the context of this film, these weapons are all symbols of the death of an age.

Pike carries a revolver on his hip, even as he discharges a machine gun into a crowd, creating corpse after corpse on a scale that the world had enver known. The same would happen a year after this film takes place, when World War I soldiers used similar machine guns, using Napoleonic tactics in a modern war. The outlaws in this movie come from a different age. They come from an age when fanning a revolver or cranking out rounds from a lever action like Navajo Joe was about as fast as anyone could gun, but that is all changing, and it's a symbolic representation of how their entire world is becoming different.

Horses aren't fast enough to outrun the law or the railroad thugs in a world where trains and cars are coming into their own. Six-shooters are about as useful as muskets against fast-firing and fast-loading semi-automatic handguns, and the death machines that are fully automatic weapons. This movie is about an era dying and the inevitable deaths of the men, and the culture that they belonged to, as that era progressed, and it's symbolized in the weapons.

In the beginning of this film, a temperance rally is going on in the town where the gang is trying to rob the railroad. The shootout is brutal, with civilians being cut down right and left, the gang using civilians as shields at times and plenty of bloody gunshot wounds. This is violence on an entirely different level than one would see in most westerns. It's hard to grab your chest and fall over when your chest has been mostly blown out of your body and it's hard to run away from very accurate and fast rifles, even if they are being operated by incompetents.

When watching this film, pay attention to how the weaponry plays into the story. Outlaws, as spaghetti westerns so wonderfully demonstrate, are as connected to their six-shooters as knights are to their swords. In this film, the men, the weapons and the life are all dying, and they're dying in a hail of gunfire brought about by mechanized warfare.

## Appreciating This Western

This western truly offers something different. It shares with Italian westerns the updating of the genre in terms of its realism and offering a view of the West that is remarkably different than what most people will be familiar with.

This is the early 20th century West. The outlaws don't quite fit in anymore, and their way of life is dying out. Even the Army has changed. In this era, they were still largely a constabulary force on the frontier, but their blues had been replaced by more practical green uniforms, their weapons were updated and they got around on trains more than on wagon trains and horseback. Everything in this film is on the verge of modernity but, given that the West was still a remote place, it wasn't quite there yet, and the growing pains are palpable in this film.

This film features incredible performances all around. The outlaws are certainly men to be feared and you had better believe they would gun you, the viewer, down as soon as they would look at you. These are criminals who are themselves on the verge of modernity: violent, bloodthirsty, without honor and totally willing to kill civilians for no reason other than protecting themselves or for their own amusement. They'll even kill one another without a second thought. There is no chivalry in them. They wouldn't play the role of the Man with No Name and help the innocent victims of gangsters get out of town under the cover of night. If those innocent victims had money, these gangsters would probably gun them down for it without a second thought.

This is a film that follows several conventions: One Last Job, The Final Ride, Blaze of Glory and so forth. The way it plays out on the screen, however, is sometimes shockingly violent and sometimes incredibly touching. This film is about watching something pass from this world and anyone who has the capacity to engage with films will have a hard time not being somehow moved by it. For the U.S., this is the death of a legendary era full of equally legendary characters. The frontier is gone, the cowboys are mostly gone and

conflict is a deadlier, bloodier and more ruthless thing than it has ever been.

Anyone who appreciates what the Italians did for westerns will appreciate what Peckinpah did for them here. This film runs well over two hours, so be sure to set aside enough time to watch it, and possibly to give yourself an intermission.

# The Outlaw Josey Wales (1976)
**Director:**

Clint Eastwood

**Starring:**

Clint Eastwood

Chief Dan George

This is among the films in the National Film Registry in the Library of Congress, and it deserves the spot. The Man with No Name may be gone, but you'll see echoes of him in Josey Wales, a traumatized solider of the Civil War who heads west. The film is popular and well regarded and it shows some strong influences from Italian westerns.

## The Plot
Josey Wales was, like many soldiers, a heroic and accomplished fighter who happened to be on the wrong side. His family is massacred by a group of Jayhawkers, pro-Union forces who operated without any code of conduct or, for that matter, decency.

Wales, understandably, joins up with the Confederates, more out of personal vendetta and the need to satisfy it than for any ideological reasons. His band of Bushwhackers becomes rather notorious but are persuaded to lay down their arms based on a false offer of amnesty from a Union captain, Fletcher.

Of course, Fletcher is lying and Wales isn't about to take the offer, anyway. The same group of men who massacred Wales's family massacre his remaining comrades, but not before Wales gets a hold of a Gatling gun and does a fair amount of killing himself. This makes him an outlaw, of course, and he heads west.

With a bounty on his head, he's not only the target of lawmen and soldiers, but also the target of anyone looking to make a quick buck off killing a wanted man. With Wales, this is not so easy a proposition. He's about as deadly as they come, able to draw and shoot faster than most men can blink, and he makes the most of these abilities as he flees.

Wales makes quite a few friends who, somewhat to his chagrin, follow him as he flees, becoming a sort of family to him. It's a diverse group, including an aged Cherokee warrior, a Navajo woman who has been cast out of her society and two women—a grandmother and granddaughter—who were nearly killed by horse thieves.

The group manages to settle at a ranch house, make peace with Ten Bears, a very intimidating—but honorable and reasonable—Indian leader and Wales manages to get his revenge on the man who led the force who massacred his family.

In the end, it's not clear what happens to Wales and he literally rides off into the sunset. He's wounded, but he's made peace, even with the man who massacred his comrades. The war is over and, if he survived his injuries, Wales is free to start living again.

## What Makes This Film Remarkable

One of the things that stand out in some of Eastwood's westerns is the portrayal of Native Americans. It's on display here, and this is one of the films where the characters, no matter what color they happen to be, are fully fleshed out as real people. It's a bit ironic, perhaps, since Wales fought for the Confederacy, but one gets the sense that it was always personal to him, not ideological, and he paid a horrible cost because of the war. Everyone died a bit in that "damned war," he says, and he wants to be done with it once and for all.

The characters he meets make this movie shine, however, and they allow Wales to evolve as a character. They become his surrogate family. Wales tries mightily to get rid of everyone that starts following him, but he can't help himself from liking them. He starts to trust them. When a Navajo woman, Little Moonlight, who he rescues from rape at a trading post, disappears, he says he misses her, but mentions that everyone he starts to like eventually goes away. On the run, when he and his other Native friend notice someone is tailing them, it turns out to be Little Moonlight, not only having found her friends, but having brought along two horses and extra supplies.

Chief Dan George plays Lone Waite, an aging Cheyenne warrior who laments his loss of "power" but who is about as crafty as anyone can be. Lone Waite provides some comic relief, but not in the buffoonish, minstrel show sense. He's a dignified character, far past his prime in life but he's a good man and a good friend. Wales takes a liking to him and values him for his intelligence, his wisdom and his practiced ability to see what others miss in the landscape around him.

While the Man with No Name was always a grudging friend, Wales is, at his heart, a good man. He's seen his share of tragedy, lost his family and is on the run, but he accepts who he is and comes to care about the other outcasts he meets.

That's not to say that this film isn't dark. It is. The West, in this film, is full of villains and ruffians, killers and bounty hunters and worse. Wales, paradoxically for a man known primarily for his ability to shoot, ends up being a force that manages to make peace. He rescues his fair share of people, but he doesn't abandon them. He acts like he wants them to get lost, but it's clear enough that it's just a front. He's a traumatized man who wears his indifference and hardness like armor, but he can't abide injustice. He's a bit like the Man with No Name when he faced Ramon: a steel plate over his heart to protect him from those who are practiced and skilled at cruelty and killing.

One of the most powerful moments in this film is the scene where he negotiates with Ten Bears, an Indian leader who has the power to let Josey and his adoptive family live or die. Wales and Ten Bears reach an understanding based on respect for one another's humanity and honor, something that Wales, and most certainly Native Americans, have not experienced from others to any significant degree, at least in their recent histories.

At the end of the film, Wales even makes peace with the leader of the men who caused all of his pain at the outset of his film. The war is truly over.

## Appreciating This Western

*The Outlaw Josey Wales* isn't a spaghetti western, but it has a lot of the same characteristics of those films and they make the film very interesting. Take Blondie and give him a bit more compassion, a reason to fight that isn't about gold but retain his deadliness and you pretty much get Josey Wales.

Clint Eastwood is so much associated with his spaghetti western roles that every time he puts on a cowboy hat, it's hard not to see him as the Man with No Name. In this film, he doesn't run away from that and, in fact, embraces and expands on it. The fact that viewers are so used to seeing him as a deadly outlaw makes it easy to believe that Josey Wales could be as deadly as he's portrayed in this film. Where Eastwood does well is in making that deadly character into a more full-fledged one, with emotions that are very human, a heart, and even a capacity to respect people based on who they are, not based on their race.

This film is very dark. The West in this film is dirty, greasy, sweaty and corrupt. The people after Josey Wales are after a man whose family was massacred and whose comrades were massacred after accepting amnesty under false pretenses. Much like the law and government behind it in some spaghetti westerns, the law here serves only its own interests and certainly doesn't protect.

In the end, however, this movie turns to be one about rebuilding and throwing down arms, and that's what makes it remarkable. The biggest victory isn't won with a bullet, but when two tired old warriors just walk away from the battle, once and for all, and move on to the future and, hopefully, to better things.

## Pale Rider (1985)
**Director:**

Clint Eastwood

**Starring:**

Clint Eastwood

Michael Moriarty

*Pale Rider* is a western that not only adds a bit of depth to a standard storyline, but does so in epic proportions. The title of the film references a passage from the Bible that is read aloud in the film and that refers directly to Eastwood's character. This is a story of revenge and retribution—and justice—and one that is incredibly eerie and likely to stick with the viewer for a long time after seeing it.

## The Plot
The plot of this film, at first glance, is as much a stock western plot as much a filthy bad guy with razor stubble is a stock character. A group of prospectors is panning for gold, looking for their fortunes, but they have caught the attention, and raised the ire, of a huge mining company that's working nearby that wants all the land has to offer for themselves.

The mining company uses all the stock tactics to drive the prospectors off their land, up to and including destroying the prospector's property and beating the prospectors themselves.

A little girl prays for something to change and, apparently, that prayer is answered in the form of Preacher, Clint Eastwood's character, who comes into town wearing a priest's collar and riding a pale horse. He is death, of course, who comes riding a pale horse in the Book of Revelation.

The stranger isn't long in dispensing some frontier justice with a nice piece of hickory. The mining company is named after its owner,

LaHood, and the owner has a sadistic and bullying son, Josh, who tries to chase the Preacher out of town with one of the mining company's particularly intimidating goons. It doesn't go well for the goon.

Amidst the Preacher's story, the story of the miners unfolds. One of the men, Hull, wants them to stick together and rallies them to resist LaHood's attempts to buy them out or drive them off. They seem to be on their own, the Preacher having ridden off.

He does return, however, just in the nick of time and puts a bullet in Josh, through his hand. A corrupt marshal comes into town—he works for the mining company, essentially—and one of his gang shoots one of the miners.

At this point, the Preacher's origins come into question. The crooks know him, but he sounds like someone who's already dead.

Preacher rallies the miners and they take out the main LaHood operation. A showdown follows, with the Preacher eventually killing everyone, up to and including Marshal Stockburn, who positively recognizes the Preacher, but doesn't believe what he sees. Hull imagines Coy LaHood tries to snipe the Preacher, but Hull guns him down first.

The Preacher rides off on his white horse, clearly never to be seen again by the miners, but having saved them from the corrupt LaHood.

**The Man with No Pulse**
The movie alludes to it and Eastwood himself has said as much: The Preacher is a ghost. He's a victim of LaHood's corruption and a spirit of vengeance. Eastwood plays him perfectly and there are some notes in his portrayal that hearken back to his spaghetti western days.

The Preacher isn't really a bad guy or a good guy. One gets the sense that, if there were other people in the line of fire of LaHood's goons, he would have helped them, too. He's a vengeful sprit and he's going to kill every single man who did him and his family wrong. The miners have the good fortune of sharing enemies with the Preacher.

The Preacher has a pattern of bullet wounds on his chest that would be nearly impossible to survive, the first hint that he's not what he appears to be. He rides the pale horse and, while it's easy at first to think that this is just a reference to him being death incarnate, it literally means that he is death incarnate.

This isn't done in a way that turns him from a ghost into some sort of avenging superhero. Far from it. He's portrayed in a way that plants him firmly in shadow, but that doesn't make it obvious that there's something supernatural about him. He is divine wrath raining down on the corrupt and he's every bit as uncompromising in dealing out justice as an Old Testament angel.

This character has some elements of the Man with No Name in that we really know little about him other than he means to take vengeance on someone. Where he comes from is really irrelevant. He's also superhuman in terms of his abilities in this film, but not in the same way that the Man with No Name is. The Man with No Name was just incredibly fast and deadly. The Preacher, it seems, cannot be outdrawn, even by death itself.

When movies want to invoke the supernatural and be taken seriously, they usually do well to keep it subtle. This makes it more believable. The Preacher doesn't drift through doors or float a few inches above the ground. He doesn't have a halo and, in fact, wears a black hat. There's just something about him that makes him not quite of this world, though he's obviously very caught up in what goes on in this world and means to make the wrong things right.

## Appreciating This Western

*Pale Rider* is well worth seeing. It's a story of people standing up against a corrupt corporation, a story about people trying to make their way in a frontier and, on top of all that, it's also a very effective western ghost story.

The West and the the western genre in general is the perfect setting for such a story. It's full of mysterious characters who drift in and out of people's lives and who are never seen again. It's full of great heroes who ride off into the sunset with a simple goodbye and who leave only stories about them in their wake.

It's also full of vengeance and, in order for that to happen, it's also full of injustice. The Preacher is the sort of character that anyone who has been bullied, stolen from or worse wishes would ride into their lives. He's there to get rid of the bad people and to open up the world to the good people who want to make something for themselves without taking something away from others. He really is a force of justice.

This film, once again, shows why Eastwood is so marvelous in the western genre. His trademark squint, poker-face expression and hard eyes make him ideal for a role as a gunfighter but, taking it one step further, it also makes him idea for a role as a dispenser of justice and a protector of the oppressed. A violent one, but an effective one, nonetheless.

## Unforgiven (2008)
### Director:

Clint Eastwood

### Starring:

Clint Eastwood

Morgan Freeman

Gene Hackman

In Eastwood's spaghetti westerns, viewers got a taste of more realistic violence in that there were consequences, but the violence was oftentimes designed to be thrilling more than anything else. The Man with No Name was the best killer out there, and watching him cut his way through adversaries made an impression. *Unforgiven* concentrates on the consequences of that violence rather than on the glory of it. This is considered by some to be the best western made to date; it took home an Oscar and is part of the National Film Registry. It is, without a doubt, a fine film, in addition to being a fine genre film.

## The Plot
Eastwood plays Will Munny. He's an experienced and frighteningly effective killer but, unlike the Man with No Name, Munny is filled with regret about his former life as an outlaw. He's taken up farming. It's not long before he gets dragged back into his former life, however.

The action starts out minus Munny, in Big Whiskey, Wyoming. A group of prostitutes are offering a bounty on two men who brutally attacked another prostitute. The film has a corrupt sheriff in the form of Little Bill Daggett, played by Hackman. Daggett isn't inclined to punish the two men, Quick Mike and Davey-Boy Bunting for their crimes, leading the prostitutes to put out the bounty.

A wannabe bounty hunger calling himself the Schofield Kid tries to get Munny to help him get the bounty. Munny is miles away from being a bounty hunter at this point. He's farming, he has a family and he doesn't want anything to do with his former life. Facing financial ruin, however, he decides to go along with the Kid.

Munny recruits Ned Logan, played by Freeman, who is also an experienced and very deadly gunfighter. Like Munny, Logan is past his prime and has a wife. He has no enthusiasm for the work, but he decides to go along.

Little Bill is more complex than the usual corrupt sheriff is. He's not particularly good at upholding the law, but he doesn't want violence brought into Big Whiskey and a gunfighter who arrives to collect the reward finds himself subjected to a beating, kicked out of town and sent on his way.

Munny, Logan and the Kid try to track down the wanted men, but their first encounter with Bill goes very badly, with an already ill Munny getting beaten by Bill and his goons.

They track down the men, but Logan and Munny just don't want to go through with the killing. The Kid is more enthusiastic, killing one of the wanted men in an ambush when Quick Mike is using the outhouse. It's not long before the reality of killing makes the Kid want to give it up.

Logan never made it home. Bill's goons caught him and killed him. The Kid isn't up to what's coming, but he heads back to deliver the money they collected to Logan's family and to Munny's family.

Munny wants revenge and he gets it.

A shootout in the saloon at Big Whiskey follows, where Munny demonstrates just how skilled a killer he is. It's not a spaghetti western shootout. It's far more brutal, more of a series of executions. Eventually, Munny kills Bill, tells the townspeople that they'd do well to bury Logan properly and admonishes them that he will be back if any other prostitutes are harmed. He leaves, pursing the life of a merchant in San Francisco and, presumably, leaving killing behind him for good.

## Violence, Regret and Humanity

This film isn't about the glory of Old West gunfighters. It takes place long past the glory days of Logan and Munny, and it mirrors what was going on in the nation at the time.

The legends of the Old West were being written during the 1880s. One character in the film, who is serving as a biographer of English Bob, the gunfighter who rode into Big Whiskey to collect the bounty and who collected a beating instead, is something of a stand-in for people's notions of violence in the Old West. He glamorizes it. He writes stories about it in which the people are legendary, transformed from being human beings in a horrific and inhuman situation to mythical figures who, no matter how many opponents they face, cannot be killed.

Munny, Logan and the Kid can also be seen as representative characters. Munny and Logan are the reality behind the façade of the Old West. They are, indeed, men who have killed many and who embodied, at one time, the glamour of the Old West outlaw. In real life, however, stories don't end neatly with rolling credits and a rousing song. These men had to stay past the credits, slowly realizing that their lives consisted of one instance of regrettable violence after another. When they do get caught up in the violence again, it only brings more regret and pointless death.

There are some truly memorable scenes in this film. In one, the Kid asks Will, following the Kid's first kill, what it was like in the "old days," whether Will was scared when he was being chased down. Will can't remember; he was drunk most of the time, something the Kid is working hard on himself.

If this western has one thing that it throws in the viewer's face over and over again, it's that the reality of the West, at least where the violence was concerned, was no more glamorous than is violence today.

When Eastwood's nameless spaghetti western character killed someone, it added one more number to the men he killed and made him even more legendary. For Munny and his comrades, the killings are visceral.

"It's a hell of a thing, killing a man. You take away all he's got and all he's ever gonna have," Munny says. It's simple and succinct, and undeniably true. Munny knows the truth of killing. The Kid has just learned the truth of it and, more importantly, he's learned that he's no killer. He feels for the man he killed, even if the man he killed was a brutal sort.

There's an awful finality to the killing in this film. Everyone who does exit the world violently had something they left behind. There aren't any paper cutout characters in this film. Even Bill, the cruel sheriff, is building a house—though not very well—and has a life he's looking forward to. Logan had a wife. The Kid wanted to become a legend and, instead, he becomes a self-loathing executioner.

In that same scene, shot underneath a cold, looming sky, Munny reveals one more awful truth that the Kid is going to have to face: We all have it coming.

## Appreciating This Western

*Unforgiven* is a very highly regarded film for numerous different reasons. First and foremost, however, it's simply a very well-made film. The characters establish themselves quickly, but continue to evolve as the audience gets to know them. As is the case in many spaghetti westerns, we get to know them in fits and starts and their natures are revealed through their actions and their words.

Munny and Logan have no enthusiasm for the task they've undertaken. They approach it like farmers killing off livestock. They know they're going to be filled with regret afterword but, to paraphrase Halpern in *A Solider of the Great War*, guilt has no place in war or on a farm. These are old mercenaries riding into battle once again, each step along the way reminding them of the men that they regret being. Each mile they tick off on the way to their destination brings them closer to a reality that they were trying to leave behind.

The Kid is naïve and boisterous. He's all talk. His vision is awful, he's not experienced and he lies about his past to make himself seem like a competent killer, but he's not. Unlike what may have been the case in many other westerns, this doesn't make him weak or a weasel. It makes him human. He's the audience, in this regard. He wants to ride with the outlaws, to be a feared man and to leave a trail of dead behind him to increase the power of his legend. What he doesn't realize, however, is that those legends are just legends.

This movie doesn't come off as a stern lecture against violence or a repudiation of what goes on in most spaghetti westerns. There's never a sense that, now that Munny is older, he's serving as a moral guardian, offering a "do as I say, not as I did" lecture to the audience. He speaks simply and directly. He's intelligent and, though reformed from his hard-drinking, hard-fighting days, he did build a skillset and a reputation that serve him well in this mess he's gotten himself into.

In this film, the West is cold and glowering, the interiors are dark and uninviting and the people, while trying to maintain some sense of justice or righteousness, mostly have an underlying current of viciousness underneath their personalities. The prostitutes want vengeance more than justice. The sheriff wants his town to be free of gunslingers and the violence that they bring with them, but he's just as violent as any of them.

Munny wants to collect the reward money to support his family, as does Logan. Will desperately wants to be a legend, but soon finds out that what he did can never be undone, no matter how much he'd like to undo it.

This film, for those who get a bit tired out on the way violence is portrayed in westerns, should be refreshing, if not exactly uplifting.

This is a movie about killers and, in the end, we find out that killing isn't so glamorous after all. It's just killing. It's unremarkable, base and horrific, in most cases and, as Munny says so eloquently, it's an act of taking everything from the person you kill.

This film is worth seeing for anyone, western or Eastwood fan notwithstanding. Eastwood does manage to be intimidating, despite the fact that he's a lot older than the Man with No Name in this film. He isn't the clever outlaw who's always a step ahead of the competition in this film. He's the old pro who's not so much one step ahead of you as much as he's simply more experienced and has done this many more times than the people he encounters. He doesn't take any satisfaction in his killing and, when he does get his revenge for Logan, it's almost procedural. It just has to be done.

This is an outstanding film by an outstanding director, full of great performances and rich with depth. It's worth seeing, and worth seeing more than once.

# Dead Man (1995)
## Director:

Jim Jarmusch

## Starring:

Johnny Depp

*Dead Man* is a remarkably strange film about a man who, as the name implies, is dead before the movie really begins. He's not outright dead, of course, but he's wounded in a gunfight early in the film and the bullet he's carrying will inevitably kill him. In the course of making his way to the Pacific with a Native American named Nobody, the protagonist becomes the subject of a manhunt and a wanted man, even though he's really just an accountant.

## The Plot

Johnny Depp plays William Blake. He's an accountant heading to a town called Machine in pursuit of a new job. It doesn't go well and, by the time he gets there, he finds out that the job has been given to someone else and ends up getting kicked out by the owner.

He meets up with a woman who ends up taking him home, much to the ire of her ex-boyfriend, when he discovers the two. Charlie, the ex, tries to kill Blake, ends up killing his ex-girlfriend and shoots Blake but doesn't kill him. Blake manages to kill Charlie and takes off out of town after stealing a horse.

Unfortunately for Blake, the man he killed is the son of the owner of the company that Blake was intending to work for. Dickenson, the owner of the company, hires some thugs to go after Blake.

Blake meets up with Nobody. Nobody tries to get the bullet out of Blake's chest, but it's very near his heart and it's going to kill Black eventually. Nobody believes that Blake is actually William Blake, a reincarnation of a poet that Nobody is particularly fond of. Nobody decides to help Blake by getting him to the Pacific Ocean, where Blake can enter the spirit world where he belongs.

Blake becomes a legend. He changes from nondescript accountant without a job to Wild West outlaw, at least judging by the increasingly high amount of money that's being offered as a reward for him. Nobody turns out to be a man with a very interesting past, having been to Europe and since returned home. Nobody was taken to Europe by force, where he was shown off to curious Europeans. When he returned, he had no real place among the Native Americans, either, leading to him truly being Nobody.

The mercenaries continue to pursue Blake and Nobody, with one of them actually eating his comrades, demonstrating how particularly dangerous and cruel this man is.

Blake continues to make his way to the Pacific Ocean, killing more along the way and eventually arriving at a village. The Native Americans make a canoe for him and Nobody fulfills his goal, pushing Blake out into the ocean. The ending of this film, and the lead-up to it, is surreal and sad.

## Familiar Ideas in a New Light

The core idea behind the plot in *Dead Man* is certainly not new, but it has a twist. In many of these films, the cast includes characters who are heading west to seek fortune or fame—sometimes both— and who see the frontier as the best place to meet their goals.

In *Dead Man*, the protagonists are heading as far west as possible, all the way to the ocean. They're not headed that way to start a new life. Blake is a walking corpse from soon after the movie begins. He's heading west to die, not to live.

Nobody is a brilliant character. This film has been praised for its very accurate portrayal of Native Americans and Native American customers. You'll notice that the conversations that take place in Native American languages aren't subtitled. This was on purpose. The characters are speaking actual Native American languages and having full-fledged conversations, but they were left without subtitles so that only speakers of those languages could understand what's being said. It's interesting in terms of an aesthetic choice, but it's also interesting in what it brings to the film. As far as realistic and respectful portrayals of Native Americans, it's hard to do better than this film.

Not only are some of the lines that the Native Americans say to one another not translated, Blake doesn't know anything substantial about Nobody's favorite poet, putting the Native American character not only in the traditional guide role for a western, but also putting him in the role of the more educated of the two. This is a great facet of this movie and one that makes the Nobody character into anything but a sidekick or hired guide. He's a spiritual, intellectual and physical guide, all in one.

Blake and Nobody are very alike in that they have no place in the world. Nobody was torn from his world and returned to find that he no longer fit. He's also mixed and has no real tribe. Blake tore himself from his world—he was from Ohio—and went west seeking work, but ended up in a place where he most certainly did not belong.

The west in this film is rendered with great attention to detail. The sets, costumes and locations were all chosen to be as realistic as possible.

These details pay off. Machine, the town where Blake initially finds himself, is a dirty, dingy frontier town full of shadows and dangerous-looking characters. He looks entirely out of place. In fact, until a wholly unrealistic legend about him starts to pop up via wanted posters and his growing reputation, he really doesn't seem to belong where he is. It's too dangerous, too dark and too brutal for a man like him. The streets are full of muck, people randomly fire guns and hard stares replace hellos as the way that people greet one another.

## Appreciating This Western

*Dead Man* is not for everyone. Those who like traditional westerns will likely balk at its sometimes psychedelic and sometimes hyper-realistic nature. The film will not give you what you want if you're looking for a shoot-em-up with plenty of black-hat bad guys. It will also fail to give you want you want if you're looking for a quiet, stoic protagonist who is ultimately unflappable, even when the bullets start to fly.

This movie, however, is in love with the poetry of the West. The shooting style includes elements of film noir, with very dark shadows enveloping most of the screen at times. The characters are complex, with no real good guys or bad guys.

There's also a lot of time spent dealing with the racism of the Old West. From the train passengers casually shooting down buffalo—this destruction of the primary food source for the Plains tribes was part of the overall genocidal policies of the time—to the racism toward Nobody that he experiences from seemingly all sources, this film doesn't flinch in this regard.

This film will be memorable, even if it's not particularly appealing to you compared to other westerns. The first shootout of the movie is visceral, terrifying, and quite realistic. The rest of the movie switches between realism and surrealism quickly and without warning, making it an interesting one to watch, to say the least.

Italian westerns revamped a tired genre with a fresh look at the way that people acted, lived and died in the Old West. *Dead Man* does much the same and, though it didn't launch an entire genre, it's a good film to watch when your want to see something a bit different.

## Django Unchained(2012)
## Director:

Quentin Tarantino

## Starring

Jamie Foxx

Christoph Waltz

This film is one of Tarantino's tributes to genres past, though it stands on its own as an excellent film. Like many of his films, it features well-known actors who, in this film, go beyond the roles that they are usually featured in. It has been widely praised as one of his best but, due to the very controversial topic of the film, it has also been criticized for being insensitive to the reality of slavery. Whatever else it may be, it is pure Tarantino and, when his name pops up, there's always controversy, usually surrounding an excellent film, and this is very much the case with *Django Unchained.*

## The Plot
This movie takes place in 1858 in the American South. Django is a slave who, after being purchased by the Speck brothers, is being led to his new home on a cold night, along with several other slaves. The slave drivers transporting him are stopped on the road by a rather comical looking fellow; a German dentist, judging by the spring-mounted molar on the top of his wagon and his thin, but still noticeable, accent.

The dentist, Dr. King, soon establishes himself to be more than meets the eye when he guns down the slave drivers with the lightening quickness and emotional distance characteristic of spaghetti western protagonists. He frees Django, gets him a horse and offers him a deal. Django helps Dr. King identify two wanted men—King is a bounty hunger—and Django gets his freedom and a cut of the bounty. King happens to find slavery disgusting, so his actions, at this point and thereafter, are rooted in both his profession and the fact that he not only cannot abide slavers, but he genuinely hates them.

Django, understandably distrustful at first, warms to Dr. King as he finds that the man is sincere and gradually starts to define himself as a character, quickly becoming the lead in the story. Django first sees how slick Dr. King is when he arranges for a sheriff to kick the pair out of a bar, then guns down the sheriff in the street. When the marshal shows up, Dr. King presents a warrant for the man and the written authority to bring him in dead or alive.

Over the course of the film, Dr. King becomes Django's mentor after discovering that Django has a natural talent for handling a gun and a remarkable intelligence. The two become friends and, after Django tells Dr. King the story of how Django and his wife were sold to separate slavers as punishment for trying to escape the plantation they were formerly at, Dr. King starts to see Django as something of a hero. Django's wife happens to be named Broomhilda and is a fluent German speaker, which gets Dr. King even more interested. He agrees to help Django as the story so closely parallels a famous German legend.

Over the following winter, the partners bring in a lot of money on bounties, with Django's skill increasing all the time and Dr. King both helping him become a better bounty hunter and helping him to learn to read. By the time the winter is over, Dr. King is ready to help Django rescue Broomhilda, something Dr. King seems to be aching to do.

Broomhilda is owned by a deranged and brutal plantation owner named Calvin Candie. He owns a plantation called Candyland, is very much a Southern dandy and delights in appearing French, though he doesn't speak a bit of it and gets embarrassed if this is revealed in conversation. He's a vain, ruthless and entitled man; one who fights slaves to the death in what are, in the film, called Mandingo fights.

Dr. King and Django—now using the name Django Freeman—convince Candie that they are looking to buy a slave for fighting and that Django is a black slaver who happens to be an expert in Mandingo fighting. Django manages to hold back his disgust, both at the role he has to play and the people by whom he is surrounded, long enough to find Broomhilda.

A particularly sycophantic and sadistic house slave named Stephen becomes convinced that Django and Broomhilda know one another. He exposes the two by humiliating Broomhilda in front of Django. Django and King had originally agreed to pay $12,000 for a top-notch fighting slave and were pretending to want to buy Broomhilda because King had no one else to speak German to and he liked her company. When they are exposed, they agree to pay $12,000 for Broomhilda and, it appears, they may be able to walk away with Django's wife.

Candie becomes more sadistic and, after taunting King with a demand of a handshake on the deal, King loses his patience once and for all. He shoots Candie through the heart, setting off a gun battle in which Django manages to kill most of the overseers and other thugs on the plantations. He ends up getting captured, however, and nearly castrated, before being shipped off to a mine company to die as a slave at the suggestion of Steven.

He escapes the slavers from the mine, rides back to the plantation and exacts revenge in spectacular fashion.

By the end of the film, Django is a full-fledged western—or southern, as Tarantino termed the film—hero, riding away into the night with the woman he loves, dressed to the nines and leaving only the ashes of Candie and his horrific operation in his wake.

## The Controversy

Predictably, a lot of the controversy surrounding this film is concerned with the use of racial epithets, particularly the n-word, which is used literally hundreds of times throughout the film. Of course, this is set in the antebellum South, making this an entirely realistic use of language of the time.

Several other sources regarded the film as controversial due to slavery and the massive scale of human suffering associated with it being used as entertainment, though that's a subjective interpretation of the film.

The film does have very unpleasant moments, to be sure, which should come as no surprise to any viewer. It's set in an era when one of the most shameful episodes in U.S. history was taking place, on a plantation owned and run by a sadistic racist who genuinely seems to regard slavery as something to be enjoyed, rather than just profited from.

This movie is ultra-violent. Again, there's no real surprise there. This is a Tarantino film and the man is not known for having a tendency to shy away from violent content. In fact, he revels in it more than anything else and that is on display in *Django Unchained.*

There are many reasons why people find this film to be controversial or offensive. Probably the best way to approach this film is with a realistic attitude. If Tarantino's other films were offensive to you, *Django Unchained* will probably offend you, too. If you're a fan of Tarantino's work, you'll likely very much enjoy this film. Love his work or hate it, Tarantino does know how to make a movie and this one very much carries his trademarks.

**A Tribute, Not a Pastiche**
To say that *Django Unchained* borrows from spaghetti westerns is understatement in the extreme. The film opens up with the theme from the original *Django*, already profiled in this book, but with a shot of slaves marching in chains behind it.

The film is very much a tribute to those films. Like those films, it ratchets up the violence beyond the norm, even for modern movies. The result is sometimes comical, sometimes gut-wrenching. When people get shot, their blood explodes out of their bodies as if they were an aerosol can full of movie blood. People die right and left, and in very gruesome and graphic ways, but it's easy to see why this is the case.

Those spaghetti westerns, when they first came out, shocked people with the violence and darkness they put up on the screen. Shocking an audience with violence is not easy to do today, as by even the '80s action movies and slashers had become so graphically violent that, today, one full generation from that era, viewers are not likely to even notice violence unless they really see a lot of blood and a lot of pain. Tarantino delivers on both.

This film also plays true to the strong, silent hero in spaghetti westerns in Django himself. This character is a bit more complex, however, keeping the film from veering into pastiche territory. He's a man with a made-up name—the Freeman part, at least—not a man with no name. He has a history, and that's what drives this film and defines his character.

This character also plays true to Italian westerns in how it treats the most obvious issue it's addressing: race. In Italian westerns, as has been said, Mexicans were not ignorant peasants and Native Americans were not noble, or ignoble, savages, in most cases. In this film, Django is not freed by a white man who risks everything to do what's right. He's freed by a white man who needs someone to identify a fugitive, and who finds out that Django has a lot of ability as a marksman, as well as a lot of courage and makes an excellent partner. Dr. King is not symbolically making up for white injustices against black people by freeing a hapless slave. Dr. King is, quite simply, too intelligent and compassionate to be a racist and too good of a businessman to pass up on a partner who can make them both very rich. He does say he feels some responsibly for Django, since he is granting him his freedom, but this is not a father/son type arrangement. Quite the opposite.

Dr. King sees Django not only as a hero, but as a very important hero in Germanic myth: Siegfried. Siegfried, according to the tale, had to rescue Brunnhilde—the actual spelling of Broomhilda—from imprisonment at the hands of Odin. He was a typical hero of epic tales, literally fighting dragons and getting through a ring of fire to rescue Brunnhilde. Dr. Kind sees Django as this character, and as a German, he cannot pass up on a chance to help the real-life Django complete his quest.

Django doesn't fall into the trap, as a character, of imitating a white hero. He's his own person. He's hard, can be ruthless, but has a sense of justice that drives him and, even more so, is driven by love. This takes him miles away from many other spaghetti western characters, which were oftentimes trying to add more gold to their stash or trying to avenge a death with yet more death.

Ultimately, however, this film succeeds in playing tribute to Italian westerns in that it is just plain cool. Django is cool. Dr. King is cool. Broomhilda is cool. These characters are likeable, fun to watch and have an incredible story in which they take part.

If you love Italian westerns as much as Mr. Tarantino does, you'll likely love the hero that he created in Mr. Freeman.

## Appreciating This Western

Turn off the Internet controversy machine and just put *Django Unchained* in your player and make up your own mind. Will it offend you? Maybe…probably. Will it be worth it? Most definitely yes.

This film takes something that is very hard for Americans to talk about and re-contextualizes it as the background for a hero to emerge. This led to a fair share of the criticism that Tarantino faced, but, notably, almost no one levels those types of criticisms on war movies set during World War II that use the Holocaust as a backdrop to show how heroic the Americans were.

If you love spaghetti westerns, you'll probably get *Django Unchained*. Like those moments, it has moments of genuinely funny comedy—proto-Klansmen being foiled by their own ill-made hoods, for instance—and moments that are genuinely painful to watch. It has hateful, evil villains and heroes who aren't exactly good guys, but who you'd most certainly like to meet and would have nothing to fear from.

This truly is a spaghetti southern. Whether you end up loving it or turning it off minutes into it out of feeling offended, you won't forget it, and it's a great film all around.

## Further Recommendations

The films listed in this book constitute a fine selection of spaghetti westerns, but there are many more out there. You'll find stories similar to those told in the other films listed in this book listed below, and there are still plenty of others to choose from.

Many of the films in this genre have several different titles, which can make them difficult to find. There are also plenty of them that are hard to find on streaming sites or on DVD, and you may have to do some hunting around. Sometimes it's worth it, and there are DVD releases of these films coming out all the time.

When you do look for new films to check out, be sure you check the free streaming sites for legal copies of films in this genre. Not all of them had their rights secured, so some are in the public domain and, as *Death Rides a Horse* demonstrates, films in the public domain are sometimes very good. There's no piracy involved in doing so and no one's being cheated when you watch public domain films, so you're not crossing into outlaw territory by taking advantage of the fact that, sometimes, someone just forgets to lock the rights down.

## The Mercenary (1968)

Directed by Sergio Corbucci, the same man who directed *The Great Silence*, this film is similarly dark, but nowhere near as bleak as *The Great Silence*. It also features heavy political themes, being set against the backdrop of the Mexican Revolution. It has a Morricone score.

## Companeros (1970)

The third in what some consider a trilogy of sorts by director Sergio Corbucci, this is a part of the Zapata western subgenre of spaghetti westerns. This film also mixes political messages with a story centered on the Mexican Revolution, and is one of the best-known films by this director.

### *Matalo!* (1970)

The title means "kill him" and this film has some great Mexican banditos in it. It's a story filled with double-crosses and other dirty deeds and it's one to check out if you want to spend some time with bandits from south of the border.

### Duck, You Sucker (1971)

This is the last western directed by Sergio Leone. It's also got a score by Morricone, bringing two masters of the genre together for one last time. This western is set in Mexico during the Revolution. It's a typically complex Leone plot and is lined to two of his other films, *Once Upon a Time in the West* and *Once Upon a Time in America*. It's highly regarded, but doesn't as much attention as his other films, for the most part, making it a great one to see if you want to delve further into the obscure films of this genre.

### Shoot the Living, Pray for the Dead (1971)

This film stars Klaus Kinsky, a staple actor for this genre. It centers on a bank robbery and a double-cross, a classic plot that is well executed here. The film has a lot of overtures to film noir in it, giving it a slightly different feel than many of the other spaghetti westerns out there.

### My Name Is Nobody (1973)

This is among the westerns that deal with the decline of the West. This film follows Henry Fonda and Terence Hill, the latter of whom had made a name for himself in Italian westerns and the former who was already a huge star, as Hill's character tries to convince Fonda to relive his glory days as a gunfighter.

### Django's Great Return (1976)

Django's back, sort of. It's really just original Django actor Franco Nero who plays a character who comes home from serving in the Civil War. This is a very-late-in-the-game entry into the genre and the old horse that is the Italian western genre is showing a bit of its age at this point. Nonetheless, this movie has some excellent scenes in it and is well worth seeing. The plot will be familiar to anyone who has delved into this genre but, as always, when it works, it works very well and it does work in this film.

## The Trinity Films

These films included two, *They Call Me Trinity* (1970) and *Trinity Is Still My Name* (1971), that were widely copied after they came out. These were comedies that did very well at the box office. The second of the two, in fact, held the box office record for Italian films when it was released. These films are raunchy, slapstick comedies that play on some of the most common elements of spaghetti westerns. They feature impossibly fast gunfighters, of course, but take it to the level of ridiculous on purpose.

## The Big Gundown (1966)

Lee Van Cleef is back and a bounty hunter in this film, the title of which leaves little doubt as to what's in store. The film follows the bounty hunter as he tracks down a rapist, who may actually not be the biggest villain in the story that Van Cleef's gotten himself wrapped up in. A classic tale but one whose execution is generally considered to be very good.

**Conclusion**

The films mentioned in this book, and the many other films in this genre, offer something unique in movies. They exist in a genre that had become predictable and that was becoming outdated when they were in their prime. The reinvented that genre, however. They made it new again, and more interesting, for the most part.

They also represent taking something that's nearly synonymous with the U.S., the Old West, and putting it in the hands of European directors and actors. This resulted in a very interesting perspective on the era, the people in it and the harshness of the frontier.

In American westerns, for the most part, there's something optimistic at play. Whatever troubles the characters are facing, they're troubles that are destined to become part of legend. These are the pioneers, the cowboys, the explorers and so forth. In Italian westerns, the people on the frontier aren't so much part of a legend as they're trying to make it through life on a day-to-day basis. There are few heroes in these movies. Villagers, for the most part, look like they have lives of drudgery, hardship and isolation. Justice is corrupt and, when it's not, mostly arbitrary. Heroes are usually antiheroes. In spaghetti westerns, the violence is sometimes on the most epic scale of all, and brutality is easy to come by.

The antiheroes in these movies are much closer to the protagonists of today's films than were the heroes of the early cinema westerns. These are hard men and women, tough, violent when they need to be and perfectly comfortable with violence as a normal part of everyday life. These characters, even though many moviegoers today may not have seen them before, have endured in today's characters and films. Quentin Tarantino is mentioned several times in this book. Watch his films again after seeing a good selection of spaghetti westerns and you'll recognize his high regard for the genre. Eastwood's Man with No Name character exists in most of his western roles that followed it, in many regards.

If you're interested in more of these films, the good news is that they have a very active cult following. They also have a healthy following among mainstream moviegoers, the Dollars trilogy being three of the most well-known and popular of this genre. There's a lot more to explore here. Some of the films are definitely better than others are, but there's much more to explore off the beaten path, and it's worth it to take a risk on this genre now and then, because it tends to be very good.

## Photo Credits & Sources

By not listed (Cramers Art Rooms of Cherryvale, Kansas) [Public domain], via Wikimedia Commons

By HombreX at en.wikipedia [Public domain], from Wikimedia Commons

Georges                        Biard                        [CC-BY-SA-3.0 (http://creativecommons.org/licenses/by-sa/3.0)],    via   Wikimedia Commons

By movie studio (eBay) [Public domain], via Wikimedia Commons

By Trailer screenshot (Slim trailer) [Public domain], via Wikimedia Commons

By Giulio Petroni (Screenshot from movie) [Public domain], via Wikimedia Commons

By Studio (Hollywood Memorabilia.com) [Public domain], via Wikimedia Commons

Jack Palance and director John Badham during filming of "The Godchild." It was filmed in 1974 at Edwards AFB. Source: [http://www.edwards.af.mil/gallery/html_pgs/showbiz4.html Edwards Air Force Base] {{PD-USGov-Military-Air Force}}

Georges                        Biard                        [CC-BY-SA-3.0 (http://creativecommons.org/licenses/by-sa/3.0)],    via   Wikimedia Commons

Thomas Peter Schulz [GFDL (http://www.gnu.org/copyleft/fdl.html) or CC-BY-SA-3.0 (http://creativecommons.org/licenses/by-sa/3.0/)], via Wikimedia Commons

By Cavarrone at the Italian Wikipedia project. [Public domain or Public domain], via Wikimedia Commons

{{BotMoveToCommons|it.wikipedia|year={{subst:CURRENTYEA R}}|month={{subst:CURRENTMONTHNAME}}|day={{subst:CU RRENTDAY}}}} The tool and the bot are operated by User:Jan Luca and User:Magnus Manske. == {{Original upload log}} == This file was original

By Giulio Petroni [Public domain], via Wikimedia Commons

By Giulio Petroni [Public domain], via Wikimedia Commons

By Giulio Petroni (http://10kbullets.com/reviews/death-rides-a-horse/) [Public domain], via Wikimedia Commons

By Giulio Petroni [Public domain], via Wikimedia Commons

http://upload.wikimedia.org/wikipedia/commons/2/2b/Wild_Bunch_ Peckinpah_%26_Holden.jpg

http://upload.wikimedia.org/wikipedia/commons/7/71/Wild_Bunch_ still_opening_scene.jpg

http://upload.wikimedia.org/wikipedia/commons/f/fa/Wild_Bunch_ Agua_Verde.jpg

http://upload.wikimedia.org/wikipedia/commons/e/ed/Ben_Johnson_ The_Wild_Bunch_publicity_photo.J